Edward Dahlberg

Edward Dahlberg: A Tribute

Essays
Reminiscences
Correspondence
Tributes

Edited by
Jonathan Williams

A TriQuarterly Book

David Lewis, Inc./New York

This book first appeared as TriQuarterly 20, Fall 1970

Copyright © 1970 by Northwestern University Press
All rights reserved. Library of Congress number: 74-134302
S.B.N. 912012-10-2
Printed in the United States of America

The Editors wish to dedicate this *Festschrift* to the memory of Sir Herbert Read, who had intended to participate—"when the voices are lifted in affectionate tribute, mine will be one of the loudest."

Preface

Essays

Reminiscences

Correspondence

A garland of tributes

Poems, photos and paeans

Bio-bibliography

Appendix by the Festschriftee

Edward Dahlberg

JONATHAN WILLIAMS: *How to roast a Festschrift,
as well as how to cook a phoenix*

I write poems that are laconic as pebbles, so when it comes time to write prose I like to pull out all the stops and do a lot of throat-clearing and ground-pawing, like Anton Bruckner, another rusticated, mountainous person. By the time this *Festschrift* of ours is published it will have been struggling toward print for three whole years, which is *adagio* for sure. I sent out the first letter of invitation on April 28, 1967. (Here it is important to acknowledge the facilities of the Aspen Institute for Humanistic Studies, afforded me during tenure as a scholar-in-residence. I could never have done the editing without Rosinante in the form of a trusty xerox machine.) Still, the date we were really aiming for was July 22, 1970, the seventieth birthday of Edward Dahlberg; and through the good offices of Charles Newman and the others at *TriQuarterly,* we may come close. Publication will come as a particular relief to Dahlberg himself, who must have thought often that I was trying to make it a posthumous tribute. As I give some of the reasons for the *adagio* tempo, I recall Charles Olson, at his quietest and most personal moment in "Maximus, to Himself," saying: "I have had to learn the simplest things last; and, we are all late in a slow time. . . ."

Note, please, this passage from C. E. Vuilliamy's *English Letter Writers:* ". . . the arts of talking and writing in a familiar style have lamentably decayed, and the causes of decay are evident enough. Speedy communication, the hurry of life, complexity of employment, diversity of distraction, the press and the radio and the television,

5

increased irritability, a common resolve (it would seem) to destroy or contaminate all the sources of quiet, these are the factors which have now expelled our social graces and accomplishments." Few under thirty will know what a social grace is; few over thirty will have given them thought for years. I recall, for example, once receiving a printed-form postcard from Edmund Wilson. He had simply checked one of a series of numbered responses like: "Edmund Wilson cannot answer your letter because (1) it bores him excessively; (2) he is too busy studying the later symphonies of Morton Gould; (3) he finds you impertinent for writing in the first place; (4) he is spending the summer in Cumberland making dandelion-and-burdock mineral water for Christmas presents for bilious belles-lettrists." Etc.

So it was fairly stupid and sanguine to think that I was going to come to much but considerable grief by asking more than 125 writers, poets, editors, publishers, critics, realist painters, photographers, booksellers, mavericks, et al., to contribute to a *Festschrift* for Edward Dahlberg. If you ask 125 battered literary people for *anything,* 100 will take issue with you and insist that you were totally wrong to begin in the first place. And here I was asking writers to bury the hatchet—when Dahlberg has buried it in more writers' skulls more often than anyone else living! Does he not say every day of his life: "I reflect the age to which I am opposed. . . . It does not matter how often I fail; what is important is that I never joined the intellectual or the academic crowd. The rabble esthete is no better than any other species of a demagogue, or what Prior calls the comma and colon men. Every time a bum-bailiff of our venal, literary agora praises a bad book he starves the writer of a good one. . . ." There is nothing like such a red flag to rally the curmudgeons. Robert Bly shot back at me: "Dahlberg often tries hard to tell the truth—as his recent essay on Hart Crane makes clear again—and he deserves something better than a pile of 125 marshmallows." The always sagacious, always bilious Peter Yates replied with a parody: "I respect this aged one to whom I am opposed, who celebrates repeated failure—power to his courage!—who takes pride that he has always gone wrong on his lonesome. A rebel esthete, capable of comma and colon: I refuse the put-down by this demagogue of self-pride. He abuses easily who praises only what agrees with him. May more years widen his wisdom." Maxwell Geismar demurred: "I don't like to make judgments on literary figures I don't really know, but I do wish the volume and Edward Dahlberg all the best. All such endeavors are commendable and good for art. (Or are they?)" Edmund Wilson (actually) wrote: "I never contribute to these symposia, but have written about Dahlberg in my *Shores of Light.*"

6

Some on the list confessed to antipathy or to a lack of strong feelings about Dahlberg to back up any statement. Or, simply, a lack of adequate reading. Arthur Uphill, the London bookseller, put it amusingly: "I am sure that your proposed collation of tributes to Dahlberg will be uniquely prepared for the delectation of the public (although the public's appetite for the works themselves appears not to be insatiable), and I am flattered to be invited to provide the herbal hint to the general consommé; but for this feast I have no herb from my window box to offer, for I have, as you know, no garden, and even had I the soil to till, no plant from Dahlberg seed would grow in it. Which is to say that, after three attempts to read one of his works from cover to cover, I would be a fraud, or worse, to appear in the book." Christopher Logue complained that his liver had revolted and turned him the color of saffron and that the doctor did not include the tart Dahlbergian savories in his recovery diet. Stanley Young had to beg off because he was off on a long cultural mission in Eastern Europe. Etc., etc. Still, the point was to establish a great range of comment; i.e., *positive* response to the work—not nit-picking and bitchery—so I asked many persons whose reaction *might* be of use. I am sorry to have had no word from many who might have wished to make a contribution. The postal service, being what it has become, may well be the culprit in some cases, not the evils outlined by Mr. Vuilliamy early in this note. Yet the final response *has* been remarkable. I trust it will be of some comfort to our subject—and an evidence that a measure of camaraderie and respect for the craft is possible at a time when letters and men of letters are much endangered. (By the way, it should be noted that the *Festschrift* received asphodels via the Angelic Messengers in the name of Ford Madox Ford, Sherwood Anderson, D. H. Lawrence, Theodore Dreiser, Hart Crane, Stieglitz, John Hermann, Randolph Bourne, Marsden Hartley, Carnevali, Kenneth Fearing, Robert McAlmon, Bob Brown, and William Carlos Williams.)

Edward Dahlberg says we write to understand ourselves better and to gain affection. (He also says: "Every friend I ever had has been the fox that spoiled my vines.") One can only hope, then, that this *Festschrift* gains affection for Dahlberg and does not simply harm him. The mordant will argue with me on this. But I am too stubborn not to argue back. I tire of the New Plastic Humility—of Mr. Auden's remarking in a spate of interviews in such places as *Holiday* and *Esquire* that "in the end, art is small beer indeed"; that the only important things for a writer are earning a living and loving his neighbor. . . . And I tire of pinchbeck American journalism that can dismiss a writer of Dahlberg's stature with *two,* precisely two, paragraphs, such as those by one Alden Whitman in the daily book section of the *New York Times*. Mr. Whitman notes that *Because I Was Flesh* made "entertaining" reading several years back. An odd adjective, that. Perhaps he feels that Grünewald's "Isenheimer Altar" is likewise entertaining? He then empties the gun as quickly as a commercial on TV: "Dahlberg is outrageous, a deliberate striver for shock value, a magpie who delights to show off his gleanings from the classics, a bombast on occasion, a writer of ponderous nonsense and almost insufferable ego." It's the sort of blather used to attack a Blake, or a Whitman, or a Melville.

Let Edward Dahlberg have the Last Word, for he will in any event: "I abhor the cult of the same that is the universal malady today, and acknowledge I'm different, since I came into the world like the four elements: emotion, strife, remorse, and chagrin."

Jonathan Williams
"Pear Tree Bottom"
Hamstead Marshall, Berkshire
England
December 1969

At nineteen I was a stranger to myself. At forty I asked: who am I? At fifty I concluded I would never know.

Know thyself is a wise Socratic exhortation, but how is it possible? Do I even understand a tithe of my nature. In truth, I know nothing about anybody, least of all about myself. No matter what I do it is likely to be wrong; one bungles everything, for the brain is feeble and intuition is a saline and marshy guess. Whatever one is done he will do; that is his character, and he can neither improve nor escape it.

Who is wise, except by accident? When I am intelligent I am startled; should I be as melancholy as Avernus I am baffled. Making ready for an agreeable conversation with a friend, a seizure of unexpected spleen overtakes me. Then there are strokes of idiocy and the unreasonable gales of mirth. Who can fathom those blowsy hours of vacancy, or say unto himself: this moment I propose to be meditative? As for my paltry virtues, there is no looking glass in which I can observe them.

Now sunset writes for me, and rain scribbles my woe. I cannot revel my life. I walk upon my hurts which readers entitle my books; what else, then, can this memoir be but an enchiridion of my chagrins and shames?

Edward Dahlberg

The roots of the style grip strongly into Sir Thomas Browne, Donne, Florio, Burton, Walton, the Jacobean Bible translators; and the desire for aphorism and epigram is both classicist and eighteenth century, although Edward Dahlberg is wittier and less complex than Franklin and more involved in cadences and paradoxes of language. "Acquire one enemy solely to know someone cares for you" is warmer and more vulnerable than Franklin. "If you meddle in other people's marriages you may lose a friend but acquire a wife," "If boys do not grow into men, all our women will be children," and "How naive a man feels when he admits that he is depraved" have the complexity of a twentieth-century struggle to place sex once again at the disposal of fertile morality. Dahlberg's aphorisms turn forced and aloof in rhetoric under the weight only of the necessity of energizing platitudes. But this is not often. He has little of the explosive simplicity of Blake but resembles him in his urge toward resurrecting the body from despair. Those maxims from *Reasons of the Heart* run across a ground-base of pessimistic knowledge that life is erected on sensuality, the price of desire. Passion is a fact not to be romantically redeemed. It is neither good nor evil: "What man's head would do is always defeated by his scrotum." Blake would never have said *defeated*. "Every time a man has a thought he dies a little, and his prepuce dwindles. . . . It is more important to be a dupe than to be Timon; a man who cannot be decoyed is shrewd, which is icy insanity": there is the balance Dahlberg works on, and it is far less lonely than at first might appear. The other, social, man is here: "Do not chide a friend—stroke his heart gently. . . . To eat alone is to make a cold tomb of one's belly and to sleep by oneself is to die twice." And in *The Flea of Sodom,* knowledge and love are firmly grounded in the unpredictable: "What is truth? asks my bowels, and who made beauty and shaped Venus, says my heart."

Dahlberg's books force narrative into a continuous auto-biographical space, and the urge to aphorism is a didactic memory-theater enacted as continual checking of experience and shaping it into a portable instrument. His apocalyptic manner is not threatening but sadly wise. He calls his poems, in 1966, after America's old name as a fabulous Asian country of which Columbus believed he had found the offshore island: *Cipango's Hinder Door.* It is a texture of scholarly allusions, abrupt advice, and stays against confusion, in prose and verse, and by this date the tone warns more deliberately than ever: "The garage is a house of villainy, and there repose the carcasses of iron and tin" (in *The Flea of Sodom* this was "The garage proletariat will blow up the earth to make his existence less monotonous"). The hinder door of the garage-suburban is that democratic febrility that has always been Dahlberg's target: "I have no faith in a meek man, and regard anyone that shows a humble mien as one who is preparing an attack on me, for there is some brutish, nether fault in starved vanity." Like Williams in 1925, he looks for regeneration to the American renaissance of explorers, and, like Lawrence in 1923, to the primitive heritage of Indians: "Iroquois and Algonquin,/ Which means the blood we slew." The desolation present everywhere in Dahlberg's work is prominent: "I am fatherless and she, that mothered my vine, lies in Griefless Cliffs, and no Wind hears her." Those cliffs relate to Manhattan, rejected above Thirteenth Street: "Nothing thrives there but the fuller and the mercer, the furrier and the moth./I would as soon go to the house of correction,/Or be penned up in the maw of a locust,/Than leave my footprints beyond Thirteenth Street." His affair with New York is located in the Village of those Twenties celebrated in *Alms for Oblivion* and those Thirties so excoriatingly mocked in *The Flea of Sodom*. But Dahlberg's career is a dialectic between urban entrance and wilderness withdrawal, partly enforced by the negative reception of his writings until the middle 1960's. In a letter to Allen Tate he wrote: "I know I have made many craven errors, and resolved as early as '34 to be a man of letters and to be an eremite to do so."

There followed limbo for twenty years. He hardly wrote at all, but read and prepared for the second part of his career, the books since 1963. But the exile is internal, the departure of the outsider, the Ishmaelite prophet, still under suspicion at Columbia University in 1968. But on Wilde's aphorism, "To regret one's own experience is to arrest one's own development," he comments with resounding personal force: "it is a clever remark and one has to give it very close thought to see how wrong it is." Academic suspicion arises because Dahlberg follows through what he once said of Bosch: He is great "because what he imagines in colour can be translated into justice." That is, he is committed; substance and social action take precedence over aesthetics, which is, on the surface, peculiar for a writer who so distrusts the vernacular. Two statements fuse his position for us: "Character is fate and that's what writes books, not grammar, not being clever, or imagining that one is the lion or the fox." And: "When the body is false to itself, the intellect is a liar"—and there Dahlberg really does measure up to Blake.

He opposes that twentieth-century literature which reproduces the character of its fate—in his view, Joyce, Pound, and Eliot—and abstraction in the arts generally: "the lazy, sensual pleasure of the eyes. It is like music today, it makes the ears heavy and the mind sluggish." The generalizations are mistaken in particular but accurate in critical taste. His alert puritanism appears again in a letter to Josephine Herbst: "I would rather write a truthful book which might fall into the hands of two Negroes than pass another law giving this unfortunate people the right to vote in savage Mississippi . . . the bottom of the misery is not the Negro, it is America. . . . To be short, if one is to compose a poem to persuade the American to liberate the Negro, he has to compose it in a language of symbols and myths that will free the white American who is ready to emancipate the black one." Certainly this ideal advisory poem would not be a poem of urban reform but of urban demolition: "I am by nature an iconoclast," he wrote to Karl Shapiro, "but one in search of images, fables and proverbs —the wine for the aching heart."

The crux of Dahlberg is that agrarianism he epigrammatizes for Sherwood Anderson: "I am a medievalist, a horse and buggy American, a barbarian, anything that can bring me back to the communal song of labour, sky, star, field, love." Like Henry Adams, he believes that utilitarianism and machine technology have ousted intuition and female power with disastrous consequences. If America is Rome, borrowing legalistically and utilitarianly from Greece, then "the difference between the Roman and the American empire," he writes in *The Leafless American* collection, "is that we are now adopting the licentious habits of a Poppaea or a Commodus, or a Domitian, without having first acquired the stable customs, deities, or a civilization. And we are about to become a soldier nation without any real knowledge of Europe, Asia or the Orient." The symbol of energy in Adams purred in the Hall of Dynamos; in Dahlberg it is the deathly asceticism of the supermarket:

Go into one of those vast sepulchral supermarkets, where people hardly talk to one another, and where self-service prevails, and you quit it more wormy than Lazarus. After one has brought canned peas, or pallid, storage carrots wrapped in cellophane as the dead Pharaohs were garmented in papyri, you go to the cashier. Often a sour, wordless man or woman drops the coins into the palm of your hand so as not to touch it. But unless we exchange human germs, or otherwise we dare not kiss our mother, father or wife, we will expire, diseased and cankered, in absolute solitude.

If this description is more "symbol and myth"—and even private neurosis (canned peas can be decently cooked, germs disastrously exchanged, and conversation with a cashier an insult on both

13

sides)—it certainly focuses Dahlberg's loathing of the abstract, the undifferentiated, and the unsociable. Introducing *Bottom Dogs* in 1929, Lawrence held Dahlberg as an extreme case of the American fragmentation of community into cellular selves, "grains of sand, friable, heaped together in a vast inorganic democracy," repugnant to each other, and destroying Whitmanian "adhesives." In actual fact Dahlberg resisted, with "a strong, stony will-to-persist," the last motivation of the actual and mythical orphan who was to become for many years the Ishmael of American letters, with a will-to-persist which took the form of a self-created style. Beneath the underdog lay the bottom dog who anarchistically made himself in self-defining prose. He entered the Twenties as literary artist, but reluctantly.

His intellectual life really began, after twenty-odd years of boyhood traveling with his itinerant hairdresser mother in the Middle West and after the Cleveland orphanage and life as a box-car hobo, in the Twenties when he met Alfred Stieglitz, Dreiser, and Randolph Bourne, read American literature, and decided that in spite of everything America would have to be his "mare's nest and fate." It is as if he chose his character and fate and remained internally expatriated: "Let us admit," he begins *The Flea of Sodom,* "going over the Atlantic was a tragic mistake." His Twenties experiences are presented in *Alms for Oblivion,* like the Thirties in *The Flea of Sodom,* as a moral tract for the times, for the Fifties and Sixties, in a style which moves between high rhetoric and critically affectionate gratitudes. The style is elaborate but the moral bases simple, with their roots nourished, as always, in the Talmudists, in Buddhist writings and Greek philosophers, underpinned with reactionary American agrarianism and penetrated with the prophetic manner of Old Testament heroes. He dedicated *Do These Bones Live* to the memory of his mother, "who, as sorrowing Hagar, taught me how to make Ishmael's Covenant with the Heart's Afflictions." Dahlberg's messages from the wilderness were a series of books with dissenting purpose:

A book that weakens the will is inartistic, for all writing is heroic, feigning, imagining that though everything perish, a book will be perdurable. Knowing that death is always brushing our backs, we write to forget death.

In the opening piece in *Alms for Oblivion*, "My Friends Stieg-litz, Anderson, and Dreiser," valuable anecdotes of higher gossip gradually groom these men and others for their roles as personae in the Dahlberg drama to follow. The recurrence of the words "baffled" and "baffling" (they recur, too, in Faulkner) suggests the moral shock at the behavior of talented men to one another, and this in turn suggests their faulty sensibilities. Their stage manager curbs his hatred and self-hatred toward a larger prophetic pride, a rectitude whose style tends to be exercised at the expense of other men, even these friends. It is a style used against com-plexity and to promote stable simplicity. Dahlberg, the "neglected man," believes in men without "loose water" in them, strong, simple, potent men like Old Testament patriarchs, men who, in later essays, become "good, slow people" who write books "that enlarge our affections and trust." Ford Madox Ford's maxim, "work and more work," is "one recipe for the spirit of travail." Dahlberg is aware of the dangers of Ishmaelite pride. In a long essay on Allen Tate he formulates his temptation:

The cause of so much newfangled ignorant verbosity is, as Tate observes, the result of hubris; the misuse of words comes from the doctrine of pride.

But what fascinates him more is the dialectic of meekness and weakness with pride. He centers his critical affections and watch-ful stoicism on an emphatically masculine ideal. Dreiser is mother-dominated in spite of his strengths; Hart Crane is, like Billy Budd, a Greek boy; Whitman, Poe, Melville, and Thoreau are solitarily inclined to weak celibacy; Dreiser, Stieglitz, and Marsden Hartley are "fatherless men, without the essential masculine force to love people." While this kind of criticism describes a fear in himself, it stems also, like Leslie Fiedler's similar analysis of the feminin-ities of American male writers, from a strong Jewish bourgeois feeling for the simple stability of the family, where masculinity means becoming and being a father (it is there in Odets' *Awake and Sing!*, for example). For all his zoological appreciation of men, his flora and fauna perceptions of the human, so beautifully fused in *The Sorrows of Priapus*, he is finally compassionate and involved in the human condition. His pride may at times be a provoking arrogance or self-righteous archaicizing; more often it is salutary.

In "Word-Sick and Place-Crazy" the anti-American shape of his criticism is clearest, if rather shrill. The poet today is "no longer homely and plain about simple and plain things" but more like William Carlos Williams, who "gives us skill and invention in the place of the Cana marriage wine." This may seem an extraordinary criticism of the poet of *Paterson,* but for Dahlberg he is another "watery man" and "Heraclitus said that too much moisture is death to the soul." Dahlberg's criterion is "reliability"—"a poet ought to be one, to have a single deity that wills and purposes for his whole nature." The American poet—and Lawrence noted the duplicity of American classic literature—is a "chameleon" with "double moral hands." Art and ethics should be, as they are for Tolstoy, one and single. We must know false from true in a poet. He must give us health or "all this sick water-verse will drive us mad." The theory of this appears in "The Wheel of Sheol," in *The Flea of Sodom:*

The soul is a circle half of which is water; in this portion are the emotions and the waters of Styx which when moving yield up intimations of death, and which, when not abated by the understanding that is in the dry part of the soul, destroy the will. In the dry regions there is a growing Vine which is the faculty of learning upon which the pard, the lion and the wolf raven. Only when the dropsical flood of Acheron in the wet part of the spirit has somewhat diminished, and when the three beasts are asleep at the root of the Vine, can man eat and know.

A poet is to have one character, a singleness which will prevent "dreary pluralistic morals" and produce at least "clear" style and form:

Thoreau and Williams are frontier minds, with an acute wind-and-bramble logic of the physical ground, but all earth is not suitable habitation for the imagination. I can't talk to rocks and trees, says Socrates.

The primitivism of "raw forest and violent places," in Crèvecoeur, Cooper, Twain, and Parkman, is sickness; Williams, like Melville, is finally "just homeless, without parent, or man and woman to be near; a prey to the fiercest elements," a pair of "writing Ishmaels." Dahlberg emerges as the philosopher of the middle ground of garden pastoralism:

16

Speech, to be a deity to the people, must come from the pasture or from grain, fruits, and livestock. We must not forget that the simple is not mean or obvious but has in it such depths and gods as to be a healing medicine for the soul, the body, and the earth.

Thoreau's cultivation of simplicity and "necessaries" becomes here an emotional playing with old-fashioned romantic husbandry and threats of disaster from complex technology. Since it presents no alternative to American urban democratic industrial capitalism except pastoralism, it is a jeremiad in a vacuum, a familiar city-versus-country wheelwright's shop form of archaic puritanism: "a farm, a glebe, a plain and an elm breed charity and pity, which the fiction of the groundless city surfeit and nausea lacks." Where Blake realized the need to build the city, such commonplaces of anti-city tradition, going back to the denigrators of Babylon, lead Dahlberg to deny Williams' effort to understand and renew the city in *Paterson*. The culture of cities is most of what we measure civilization's achievements by. "Grum" anarchistic nostalgia for the pastoral is an interesting American ploy, but pious wishful thinking only increases the disaster of what cities have become. Complexity of intelligence, literary form and style, and human living do not necessarily mean degeneracy away from "simplicity," itself equally open to the abuses of tyranny, the disease of vitalism.

As for language, Dahlberg may accuse Fitzgerald, with some right, of using part of the Twenties' journalistic glamour vocabulary for other than period and atmospheric reasons, but to score off his fiction in order to boost the "bluff, barbaric vulgate" of Dreiser and others—"sometimes very nimble and very masculine" —seems odd indeed:

Their words, deriving from old manual occupations, are far more masculine and energetic than the lymphatic ones that come from advertising and from inventions that are emasculating the human faculties. A word that arouses some sort of contemplative or physical activity is good, and one that does not is base.

Such vitalistic theories of language simply ignore the fact that Fitzgerald's major heroes are fatally undernourished by American society and rely degenerately on a phony charisma of leadership and money. They are a critique of the very carelessness and ignorance Dahlberg inveighs against. But he goes into no detail. He prefers Charles Peirce's "isolated and austere words" to William James's "gregarious yokel phrases" without mentioning James's experimental refusal to use the jargon of systems, and with no sense of his courageous skeptical inquiry into every phenomenon. The radical analysis of concepts is anathema to Dahlberg, the man who can seriously write that

the plough is a sign of peaceable ground-workers, but the rubber-tire is a tool of a nomadic, apathetic class that is constantly moving away from debts, marriage and boredom,

and insists that America is a nation of "rubber-tire plebs" and "factory nihilists" whose hopes are wasted by financial patricians. It is a curiously unfactual version of the machine-in-the-garden antagonism, and needs heavy correction from something like Lynn White's *Medieval Technology and Social Change.* Back to the plough that broke the plains is not much of a call to any American who is bright enough to remember preindustrialized agricultural slavery and poverty, and the themes of Pare Lorentz's documentary film and *The Grapes of Wrath,* or to know about the condition of the San Joaquin Valley workers in the Sixties. Thoreau did suggest "how to live without wasting the human spirit," but that spirit is just as much wasted in sweat behind a plow as in a factory. But, cries Dahlberg, "what need has a man to go beyond the sheepcote, the threshing floor, and the augur's timbrel? A mortar and pestle are enough for a culture!"; and again in *The Flea of Sodom,* "there was no iron in Eden. . . . Iron appears in Jeremiah, Job and Daniel, the scriptures of weariness, and in Genesis, the lament for the Arcadia of Seth and Enoch. . . . Wood was savory in bucolic Zion."

Probably it is that Dahlberg resolves the tensions between *isolato* and *sociality* too Hebraically, so that Melville becomes a literary villain and, like Poe and Hawthorne, "the vassal of that Puritanic Beelzebub, Cotton Mather, the father of the Christian homosexual." Dislike of homosexuality penetrates Dahlberg's work, and the mother hatred that goes with it. He is tremendously conscious, as Adams and Fiedler are, of the weakness of the presentation of women in American literature, the wretched her-

18

itage of puritanism in the work of Poe, Melville, Whitman, Emerson, Hawthorne, James, Hart Crane, Eliot, and Pound. Thoreau he admires, but he, too, was a cold bachelor. The old hatred is comically shrill in *The Flea of Sodom:* "Perversity is the vice of Gomorrah. The pederast denies gnomes and visions." Homosexuality is the epitome of wateriness and the verbosity of Babel—without detailed explanation. *Moby-Dick* is "a Doomsday book about water," the central American watery book for watery men. Dahlberg ignores the meaning of the Ishmael-Ahab polarity, the analysis of religious myths and the transformations of Inner Light into heroic quest for light in whale oil, all of which should deeply concern a man so obsessed with personal integrity in action. Yet his essay, *"Moby-Dick:* A Hamitic Dream," remains a brilliantly excoriating attack on a masterpiece of what Dahlberg sees as "a Christian zoolatry, a Puritanical bestiary." But should he not admire Melville's prose, considering he writes in *The Flea of Sodom,* "simple prose is often conceived for the mind that is dead rather than quick"?

Of all Dahlberg's books it is *The Flea* that is almost pure style, to the point of rabbinical dandyism, fulfilling his own prescription:

The line is gnomic, pulsing with Ovid, Livy, Strabo, Suetonius, Herodian, Plutarch, the Book of Enoch, the Apocalypse of Baruch. The similes themselves are definitions of ancient rituals, which are a bucolic physic for men who feed and gender upon our macadam meadows.

The very control of the cyclic cadences contains an uncontrollable nostalgia for definition by style, the grand style of Milton or Faulkner or James, a pounding "camp" compounded of classical and Old Testament myth and rhetoric, in which sheer articulacy is a main antidote to those hemorrhoids which are his targeted cultural disease, much as cancer is for Mailer or Burroughs. And the Thirties were America's hemorrhoidal years, looked back to with such nostalgia today. As Dahlberg so appositely remarks of his American: "instead of piety for ancient wisdom, he has nostalgia." About the phony golden age of political commitment, he writes like a Kansas John the Baptist who knows that the Christ is a legend and that his own prophetic stance is the irritant to neglect.

He analyzes artistic and political bohemianism as monstrous parasitism. He knows the Jesus trap temptation—"Let somebody come to me for counsel, and the strength goes out of my knees"—and the Judas trap—"one glance at Judas and the flea is so tickled he crawls into your shirt." Dahlberg survived ideology in the Thirties, itself an achievement. His flea of Sodom is American spleen, the "itching Socratic tedium" of intellectuals and artists, "the dogstar, ennui." When Pilate Agenda moves into Poe's rooms on Waverly Place, it is like a betting office opening in Blake's old premises on South Molton.

Dahlberg's advice to himself is "try to be still" when "everybody is living mythically and wants to escape boiling Aetna cement"; practice the maxim, "Man must rest or walk to meditate, but not on Hecate's pavements," and not when, as even Pilate sees, "the people are half-born seminal accidents—policemen, wardens, auto-mechanics and Karl Marx clowns." Ishmael walks in a whirlpool city of perversions with the glaring sanity of the pyrrhonist:

What demon drives modern Ishmael to lands sown with cockles by windy constellations and fierce, protean seasons. . . . Ishmael in his cold ass's solitude will bite off his flesh for a soft look. The mendicants run after the low loaves and fishes, but Ishmael hungers for man. . . . Did not the Lord cast out the innocent infant Ishmael, and did he not take more delight in the identity of Jacob? . . . Man knows no more evil stroke than to walk to and fro in the earth as Lucifer does, and has no other balm for the pain in his spirit than to be still. Be quiet, my ribs; stay home, lambs and goats of Ai. Rest; the ships of Tarshish are in your room: Eden is in a chair. . . .

The vortex of New York Thirties whirls around him, while "lonely artists create pariah wisdom." But barbarism begins when the self is isolated. The Ishmaelite prophet grows "testy" as he makes his literature of "hallowed remembrance," and again the major targets are linked: "The most destructive sins in Genesis are Nimrod's Tower of Babel and sodomy. . . . The desire for Babel is the appetite for a universal, ratiocinative Gomorrah, where Ahab and Elijah, the Prophet's mantle and Nero's sacred beard, are of the same moral weight, and man and woman, wearing the clothes of sodomy, act as a single sex." The other major target is the Machiavelli who observes "that virtue and propriety beget rest, rest idleness, idleness riot, riot destruction from which we come again to good laws." Dahlberg replies: "This is the wisdom of ennui. Forms that are created by men who have not a sedentary Buddha in their soul yield the most miserable havoc and satiety." It is the young American's reply later in the Sixties to those who would perpetuate the state of the *Report from Iron Mountain.* The attacks on Sodom and Machiavelli both stem from the same source: a warning against the sterility of nondifferentiated life. But it goes ridiculously far, to a desire to return to the Ancients' "abhorrence and prohibition of public nudity." Again this is part of Dahlberg's sense of the modern degradation of the body as much as his own puritanism: "the Prophets detested the priapic beast, and no lewd goat sported with the maidens of Israel."

It is clear why he pays homage to Charles Olson, "poet of the little spermacetic sea-boke"; they both have a feeling for legend interpreted, not as metaphysics, but as ecological equation: "The Book of Job is the scripture of reason, for Uz means to counsel, and Lucifer is the fallen planet of time and the unquiet demon of ennui that afflicts Israel whose only godly receipt is to sit." Legends are Dahlberg's antidote to time. Dwellers in time "can never discern the Paradise promised by the Angel of the Apocalypse. . . . As man journeys away from Eden to those remote Boreal lands, he ravels out his spirit thinking about time. Western thought is the metaphysics of tedium and Orcus." Again and again Ishmael defines his paradise lost in terms of resistance to tedium, the flea of the alienated intellectual. The universal and ratiocinative, in their abstraction, are opposed by the distinctive, local, and pleasurable:

Jehovah confounds the tongues of men that each nation may have its own myth and names. When all races are melted into one theoretical people there will be no difference between Shem and Ham. . . . man will cohabit with man, and ennui and riot will roar in his veins like the Fires of Gomorrah.

America as the image of global melting of races is exactly the tradition Dahlberg opposes. He believes, by implication, that the discovery of Americanism in the Twenties and Thirties did not produce a distinctive culture:

> Nations without stable forms and deities are brutish. A populace, mad for
> novel raiment and bizarre amusements, breaks antique idols and proverbs,
> and canonizes trash.

Through his character Beliar, in "The Wheel of Sheol," he ex-
poses that lust and avarice for wisdom at the core of twentieth-
century power systems and their intellectual apologists, painters,
poets, and composers: that Byzantinism rife in Hulme, Yeats, and
Wyndham Lewis:

> the art of Beliar was ratiocination and glutted with circles and rings and
> the isosceles triangle which were diagrams of his lewdness.

Dahlberg is at least with the American line of Poe, Hawthorne,
and Melville in his fear of the knowledge which separates a man
from his fellowmen until his loneliness becomes criminally oppressive, the syndrome continually exposed by intelligent men, from
Marx's 1844 *Economic and Philosophic Manuscripts* to Camus'
Caligula in 1945. But obsession with time and the geometrical is,
for Dahlberg, part of the blight of change in the body of men. He
may say, "Knowledge that is not action is gross and evil" (in a
letter to Herbert Read), but by action he means stabilizing reaction:

> The lover of time is also the lover of change and of Sodom. . . . the sick-
> ness of time which is such a boiling tumour in the imagination that Beliar
> begs for death to be rid of Time. . . .

> Old customs are the weights and measures of the gods. No one can invent a
> sane habit or one good deity. . . . Novel artifices nourish insolence and
> slaughter. Zeus hanged Prometheus from the rocky Caucasus for bringing
> fire to men, and the Lacedaemonians reproved Timotheus because he added
> four strings to the lute. . . . Eden is a shepherd's culture in which there is
> no time. Genesis is the fable of the Tree of Reason which is also the Tree
> of Time that has cankered man since Eden and quiet were lost.

This is the most summary passage in Dahlberg's writings and
it concerns his total rejection of the greatest of all myths, the myth
of Prometheus, on which the humanistic Romantic liberals of the
nineteenth century centered their rejection of reactionary authori-
tarianism. The one classical myth Dahlberg rejects is that of the
Titan who would not serve a tyrant authority, of the male bringer
of fire, sexual energy, and human invention, the image of resis-

22

tance to subjective power. Before Prometheus, Ishmael seeks stability in the mother.

Because I Was Flesh is the biography of Ishmael's mother, told through the autobiographical rhetoric of a son whose great need is to monumentalize an immigrant American parent and a second-generation self as towers of individuality and failure in the wilderness of an America where every man's hand seems to be against them. The story is raised to the level of myth for a whole period of history. The immediate and realistic action of the Kansas City barbershop and the Cleveland Jewish Orphan Society is acted out before the gods Dahlberg so reveres, before the connecting archetypes of Hebrew, Christian, and Greek myths—Orpheus and Jesus, Mary and Hagar, Ishmael and Prometheus. Lizzie Dahlberg, the mother, is a Polish Jewish immigrant who deserted husband and two sons for a rake; but the handsome rake, Edward's unknown and largely absent father, is named Saul—a bacchic, curly-haired sensualist who appears as a demonic Pan in the wilderness wanderings of Hagar and her son through America between 1905 and the 1920's. In constructing this myth, Ishmael finds his vocation and justification, and is partly redeemed from isolation and bad luck.

The record of Lizzie's tenacity in the Middle West is itself valuable mythic American history. Her Star Lady Barbershop is presented with all the sensuous detail that the proud son remembered because he could not bear it. His own fleshliness torments him, and in that he is his mother's son and Saul's. Out of the three, it is the mother who endures. The father's defection precipitated the son into the hell of the orphanage his mother sent him to in 1912. Dahlberg's description is one of the most brilliant sections of his writing; it begins:

The regimen was martial; Scipio, who compelled his troops to eat uncooked food standing up, would have been satisfied with these waifs who rose every morning at 5:30 as though they were making ready for a forced march.

Edward became Ishmael number 92 in a place where brutality was a fetish. At eleven he learned the yearning of the *isolato* for home, and when he returned home and was renamed Edward, he had learned the price of stoic individuality:

23

I have not the least respect for my moral nature. I do what I am, and though I would do otherwise, I cannot.

He proceeded through his westward career—as Western Union "boy," cattle herder in the stockyards, laundry wagon man and hobo—to California, poverty, misery, and Los Angeles, that "sewer of Sodom." The inside story remained constant:

The life of the universe depends upon the pudendum. As soon as the Word was made flesh, man was unable to be quiet, or work, or think, until he had dropped his seed.

But in the West the orphan meets the magnificently portrayed center of his intellectual education, the YMCA cenobite Lao Tsu Ben, philosopher, reader, inheritor of the Emersonian Germanic orientalism of the Over-Soul, and "a lord of language, an autocrat of passion." This exemplary vagabond "fears nothing but the intellect," and it is he who persuades Edward to enter Berkeley at the age of twenty-one. But it is too late—"Was I not ignorant enough without walking the earth with several degrees?"—and he concentrates on assuaging his "sensual madness," oscillating between shaven-headed asceticism and the "imperial intellect" of a woman's body, the dialectical movement that has carried the rest of his life.

Lizzie herself manages one final hilarious courtship before her tenacious decline into old age, when she becomes "an admixture of Missouri and Babel . . . already a relic in a new world." Her son's destiny has been to celebrate her, to hunt for the fragments of his dismembered father, and to preserve his primal American relics for posterity. His career celebrates those torments of Puritan body-mind continuum which constitute a main American line, from Mather's diary to *The Naked Lunch,* a tradition of sensual watchfulness and sense of failure: "I am concerned with the beautiful failures," wrote Dahlberg recently. "When anyone refers to me as a successful author, I wince." It is no mask of arrogance. He has always been prepared to correct himself:

No one is on guard enough against his nature, for each man is dear to himself for his vices. It is sin to believe in one's character. Man is continually astonished at the moral weather of his identity. . . . Return who dares to his own truths.

24

JULES CHAMETZKY: *Edward Dahlberg, early and late*

It is surely time to stop thinking of Edward Dahlberg as the sport of American letters, whose principal achievement would appear to be his unique style. When critics today talk about Dahlberg's style, they are usually referring to his late work, his early work more often than not being regarded as a phase that he had to outgrow in order to achieve his maturity. This mature style reveals itself to best effect in *Because I Was Flesh* (New Directions, 1964) in a prose that is a-dazzle with rich metaphor, erudite allusions to religious and pagan mythologies, passionate attention to the rhythms and music of his periods. To his admirers, such as Allen Tate, Dahlberg's "formal elegance" is a vital part of his achievement (I quote from the dust jacket); to others, less enchanted, this style can often seem pretentious, arbitrary, freakish—especially when it is in the service of dubious prophecy (as in *Reasons of the Heart*, Horizon Press, 1966) and not, as in *Because I Was Flesh,* a necessary illumination of a vividly concrete center.[1] What I am concerned to state, or at least to suggest, in the short compass of this

With slight modifications, this essay appeared in *Proletarian Writers of the Thirties,* David Madden, ed., Southern Illinois University Press, 1968, pp. 64–73.

1. Dennis Donaghue, *New York Review of Books,* VII, 6, October 20, 1966, 26–27. (Review of *Reasons of the Heart.*)

paper, is that Dahlberg's mature style is a strategy for distancing himself from, and yet paradoxically possessing, the myth of his life, and that this is an endeavor he shares with, say, Walt Whitman, Augie March, and scores, at least, of other American writers and Ishmaels. The first task, therefore, is to place Dahlberg securely in the American grain; the second is to assess "the myth of his life" and evaluate its relevance and force as literature.[2]

As a necessary beginning in this enterprise, I propose to look more closely than is usual at his first two books, *Bottom Dogs* and *From Flushing to Calvary,* both in their aspects as integral works in themselves and as the vital ground against which the widely recognized achievement of *Because I Was Flesh* must be measured.[3]

Much of the slang in *Bottom Dogs* (e.g., "Those micks were surefire slingers, no spiffin'," p. 73) dates the book, threatens to trivialize it, but finally can be endured by any sympathetic reader. More significantly, much of it is written in the "rough, bleak idiom" that Dahlberg decries in his preface to the reissue of the book:

The rocks . . . rested in the diphtheria stream, like some dirty rain-cloud. He went around the pond, an old rotten raft on it, slugging against the mud like wet, floating rats. (*p. 96*)

The alley clotted with mud, night and the spud cans of grease from Peck's Quick Lunch was spread out like a broken spider web. (*p. 134*)

It can be seen how this aspect, the loathsomeness of this world, is in that "naturalistic" tradition everywhere evident in American letters between *Maggie* and *Last Exit to Brooklyn.* The rats, mud, grease, and spiders of the bottom-dog world seem to have been

2. Allen Tate set the problem, and challenge, with his usual fine precision: "Criticism as we write it at present has no place for it [Dahlberg's work] and this means that I shall probably not be able to do justice to my own admiration. Mr. Dahlberg eludes his contemporaries; he may have to wait for understanding until the historians of the next generation can place him historically." "A Great Stylist: The Prophet as Critic," *Sewanee Review,* LXIX (1961), 314–317.

3. *Bottom Dogs* was completed in 1928 and was published in 1930 (Simon and Schuster) with an introduction by D. H. Lawrence, written in 1929. All references in this paper are to the paperback edition (City Lights Books, 1961). All references to *From Flushing to Calvary* are to the original edition (Harcourt, Brace and Company, 1932).

spewed up by that same "explosion in a cesspool" so disgustedly characterized by Paul Elmer More when he contemplated *Manhattan Transfer* a few years earlier. The naturalistic impulse, so strong in the Thirties, was by no means its exclusive possession. Nor was the use of "the rude vernacular," so much favored by early proletarian realists. Dahlberg notes in his preface that he shared with other writers of the Twenties (he mentions John Hermann and Robert McAlmon) the notion that they "could not write about the midwest, Texas or Montana except in the rude American vernacular" (p. iii). Dahlberg's free use of "the rude American vernacular," combined with his predilection for the harsh bottom-dog world of America that he had experienced at first hand, suggests immediately his important position on the very eve of the depression and the subsequent vogue of proletarian realism and naturalism.[4] It is more difficult to assess fully the influence of Dahlberg upon that vogue than it is, say, that of Mike Gold, whose influence through the example of *Jews Without Money* (1930) and his exhortations in the pages of the *New Masses* is manifest. But Dahlberg's language of disgust, his imagery of rot and decay and— most importantly—his pioneering exploration of the bottom-dog milieux of flop-houses (p. 187), hobo jungles, and freight cars (pp. 191, 198) certainly places him in the vanguard of that school.[5] In his first two novels Dahlberg charted in original fashion the territory that was to become painfully familiar in so much of the radical literature of the Thirties.

There is no gainsaying this side of Dahlberg's early work—and if that were all, then he would merit, at best, a footnote to our literary history. But that is not all: what remains to be seen, and demonstrated, is the special quality of his voice and concerns.

---

4. For a first-rate discussion of how these predispositions underlay the posturing of many advocates of the new proletarian realists, from 1928 on, see Daniel Aaron, *Writers on the Left* (New York, 1961), pp. 208–212.

5. Three years after *B. D.* and one year after *Flushing,* Edwin Seaver was exhorting aspiring literary critics to go to many of those very places that Dahlberg has written about, to discover where "the strongest elements in our new literature are likely to come from." Aaron, p. 261.

What may strike a contemporary reader at once is the uncertainty of the narrative voice. There is inconsistency, e.g., in the spelling and use of the slang, and the narrator falls in and out of the bottom-dog idiom rather erratically [6]—a reflection, surely, of the author's uncertainty about his point of view toward the material at hand. And that, of course, is the crucial issue: what is he to make of the lives of his chief protagonists, Lorry and Lizzie Lewis?

These intertwined lives, this life, is the subject of his early fictions—which he more frankly calls autobiography in *Because I Was Flesh*—and it is, even in outline, an eccentric one. In *Bottom Dogs* we learn that Lizzie Lewis is the proprietor of the Star Lady Barbershop in Kansas City during the early years of the century. Lorry is her son, his paternity in doubt, who is sent off to an orphanage in Cleveland (at the behest of one his mother's suitors) and subsequently kicks about the country in an aimless way, winding up at the Los Angeles YMCA in the company of other aimless types. In *Flushing* the story centers on the last days of Lizzie. Lorry has persuaded her to move in with him in New York, where she tries to piece together a life as an eligible "widow," renter of flats, part-time homeopathic abortionist. There are important flashbacks to Lizzie's Kansas City barbershop days and to Lorry's experiences at the J.O.A. (we learn that the Cleveland orphanage was officially the Jewish Orphan Asylum). Except for these flashbacks and one brief trip by Lorry (riding the freights, of course) back to the site of the orphanage, the entire action converges upon the moving climax of Lizzie's last operation and her death.

The elements of the life are bizarre, marginal—an almost calculated study in alienation and displacement. A lady barber? A Jewish lady barber in the heartland of America in the "Teddy Roosevelt Days" (as the first chapter in the saga is called)? A Jewish illegitimate non-orphan orphan? What indeed to make of this matter, and how to come to terms with it? That is Dahlberg's subject in the early days, and if the voice is occasionally uncer-

6. For a full discussion of this aspect of the book, see Robert A. Whitelaw, "Style in the Early and Late Works of Edward Dahlberg," unpublished M.A. dissertation, University of Massachusetts, 1965.

tain, we should realize that he was pioneering territory only fully claimed in the Fifties—chiefly in the wake of Saul Bellow's Augie March, that other Jewish illegitimate non-orphan orphan from the American heartland. Augie, however, could unselfconsciously proclaim his American identity in his opening words, whereas, to Dahlberg, Lorry's life must have seemed merely eccentric. In Dahlberg's early efforts to come to grips with his subject it is too easy to see only despair or, as D. H. Lawrence says, "the last word in repulsive consciousness" (p. xvii). But this is only to see Dahlberg wearing his mask as the child of sorrows and to overlook his ambivalence: the sadness and the joy in this work, and the effort he makes to embrace both aspects in an appropriate style.[7]

In his introduction to *Bottom Dogs,* Lawrence distinguishes Dahlberg from the true tragedian who "dramatizes his defeat and is in love with himself in his defeated role. But . . . Lorry Lewis is in too deep a state of revulsion to dramatize himself" (p. xv). As usual, Lawrence's insight calls attention to something of great importance, in this case to the curious *passivity* of Lorry Lewis throughout *Bottom Dogs* and to an almost equal extent in *Flushing.* It is not true, however, as Lawrence suggests, that this condition results from mere revulsion. Certainly the rats, mud, and grease imagery, the sordid image of a world of sleazy rooms in which someone's hand is always up a woman's dress (p. 134), record the deep revulsion of the narrator toward much of Lorry's milieu. Yet much of the book reveals a narrator as elegiac as he is repulsed. The legendary figures of the orphanage, to whom he devotes chapters of his book, are after all nobodies, engaged only in petty food pilfering or desperate efforts to indulge their individuality; or the hi-jinks at the Y flatten out to a species of locker-room horseplay; and the culmination of the book at Solomon's danceplace, at which a young couple is married in a jazz wedding to the tune of "Avalon" (after which "The house howled, and made for the cloakrooms and lavatories," p. 266) may seem only the epitome of fatuousness and emptiness. Yet there is a stub-

---

7. Ihab Hassan does note the "savage joy" in these early books in "The Sorrows of Edward Dahlberg," *Massachusetts Review* (Spring 1964), V, 3, 457–461.

born sense in which none of this is just "the last word in repulsive consciousness." In the first place, much of it is funny in a zany way reminiscent of other writers inside the whale, such as Henry Miller and Maxwell Bodenheim and, more recently, the beats and the black humorists. More to the point, in the orphanage sections, in the section of Los Angeles, and under the Eighth Street viaduct in Kansas City, one is struck by the narrator's effort simply to name, and perhaps thereby claim, the elements of his experience. By the act of recording, he hopes to invest them with a kind of epic dignity, conscious always of a pathos and continuous irony in this effort deriving from their commonplace and unheroic nature. But the effort to include and legitimize and even celebrate these ingredients of what we are less embarrassed than formerly to call "an American life" seems to me to require recognition. This side of *Bottom Dogs* may best be seen in the portrayal of Lizzie—usually, as in this passage, in her own idiom:

> **Well, if God would help her, perhaps she could still sell the shop, take it easier, and become a real-estate agent, do a little speculating. It was no use, you could only make so much with your ten fingers and not one penny more. She should have seen that long ago and not slaved night and day, without a bit of sunshine, as she did. All her sweet youth blown through the window and for what? It didn't pay; she could by this time have something; but she was afraid to take chances. If she lost, who would help her? You didn't find money in the street. If you had a pocket full of money everybody was your friend, but if you were down and out nobody recognized you. Oh, well, she went on, God would help her and everything would come out all right.** (*pp. 149–150*)

Only the first chapters are devoted to Lizzie, but her emotional ambience controls Lorry and the book. When the narrator (and Lorry) is not in anguish over her irregular life, or dwelling upon her pathetically petty bourgeois values and "wisdom," he is clearly elegiac. Lorry and the narrator are not repulsed: they are in conflict over their heritage. This clash accounts for the passivity of Lorry—at times a kind of paralysis. The struggle central to and constant in *Bottom Dogs, Flushing, Flesh* is between rejection and acceptance, repulsion and love, of the mother. In *Bottom Dogs* the various elements jostle one another: the narrator is so close to an experience that seemed unique, eccentric, painful that the best he can achieve is an act of naming.

In *From Flushing to Calvary* Dahlberg closes upon his subject with more assurance. There is first of all the very much tighter structure. The action is complete, the scene more unified, the problem of mother-son identity more definitely in focus. Lorry's attraction and repulsion are dramatized in many small ways—by his fascination and despair, e.g., with her petty Machiavellian shenanigans—and in the larger plan of the book. He insists she give up her barbering and come to live with him in New York; then he abandons her (to make a pilgrimage to the orphanage in a futile effort to resurrect spiritually a deceased surrogate father), only to return to New York in time for her death.

If the vernacular and the literary tend to jostle one another uneasily in *Bottom Dogs,* they are more clearly defined and separated in *Flushing.* The narrator commits no "errors" in diction and spelling, and he divides the literary and the vernacular worlds between Lorry and Lizzie (there is some mixing: Lizzie reads five pages a day of *Tom Jones,* chiefly to get "tony" words to use in answering matrimonial ads). Lorry is more clearly a word-man and aspiring writer in this book. "In the beginning was the word," he reflects at one point, reminiscing about his time in L. A.: "metempsychosis, metamorphosis, transmigration, protagoras, transcendentalism, swedenborgianism, swedenborgian fungi . . . de profundis, out of the depths, dorian dorian the portrait of dorian gray, théophile gautier, multifarious, asphodel, santa monica, capistrano, monterey, carmel-by-the-sea . . ." (pp. 72–73). *Flushing* is Dahlberg's portrait of the artist as a young man. Unlike Joyce's young man, who had been to school to the Jesuits and who could soar above the nets of religion, country, and family by committing himself wholly to his mythic father, the fabulous artificer, to art, Dahlberg's artist is an autodidact American, uncertain about even locating his country, family, religion. At the end, he can only commit himself to the road. Lorry's final snatch of a Macabbean stanza, "triumph, triumph crowns our glorious way," is therefore a bitterly ironic commentary on his sense of defeat rather than his exaltation. The road from Flushing—the dreary wasteland of Brooklyn and Long Island flats, his America—to Calvary produces a crucifixion but no apotheosis. The death of his mother follows the death of his hopes for a spiritual father, so the artist is completely orphaned.

Opposed to Lorry's life and its crises are the long sections devoted to the rhythm and pattern of Lizzie's days. They are the book's triumph; her voice and the vernacular tradition it embodies are the real strength of *Flushing*. In a language authentically her own—and recognizably the product of an American experience—she reveals herself in all her shabbiness and glory. Her language is full of Sunday supplement and back-yard science and sophistication, the jargon and self-deception of the petite bourgeoise, the unexamined shards of a life lived close to the unliterary bone of American life. A sometime Machiavellian, a petty charlatan of homeopathic nostrums, her strength resides, finally, in her ability to accept the reality of the life she lives. She refuses to see it as irregular or odd; at whatever stage and with whatever oddball materials—the flotsam and jetsam of our urban civilization—she makes her communities. Lizzie's glory is that however much she seems to opt for money and advantage, she is always undone by her humanity: what she is really after, always, is respect, sympathy, love. Though she is the despair of Lorry Lewis, and behind him Dahlberg (we must assume), her death removes a vital force from his life and can only leave him desolate.

So the ambivalent relation to the mother is at the heart of this book. Besides the obvious Oedipal overtones, what I am trying to suggest is the cultural significance of the relationship: Dahlberg in a love-hate relationship with Lizzie Lewis' America. *Flushing* reveals a perfect tension between exorcism and celebration, an achieved dramatization of this problem. It is unjustly neglected as such, and as another document in the long tradition of American writers struggling to accommodate themselves to their complex fate.

Dahlberg has presumably repudiated these works of his suffering youth. A wholly different man appears in the later works—especially those concerned with "the dialogue with the body"—in a voice that is prophetic when it is not crotchety. Yet the subject of his widely admired *Because I Was Flesh* is obsessively the same as in the two early works discussed and, although "different," the voice reveals elements present in one way or another in them. There are, however, two chief differences. First of all, Dahlberg can accommodate without a sense of strain his acute sense of the observed world and "the rude vernacular" with his vast learning and his penchant for high style, to the enrichment of both—an accommodation that sits easily with a generation of readers trained to Augie March and his literary descendants. It would seem that after thirty years, in this respect at least, Dahlberg and America may have come of age. That is, despite the rage in his prophetic works, Dahlberg's pain in accommodating himself to his two worlds has abated; he has come to terms—verbally, at least—with his mother and his life. The chief difference, and it probably makes all the difference, is Dahlberg's process of mythicizing and so both distancing himself from, and possessing, his past. That is, by placing his mother and his America within a context of timeless literature, religion, and mythology, singularity is transformed to universality, shabbiness to glory, suffering and aspiration to aspects of man's eternal condition.

> **Let the bard from Smyrna catalogue Harma, the ledges and caves of Ithaca, the milk-fed damsels of Achaia, pigeon-flocked Thisbe or the woods of Onchestus, I sing of Oak, Walnut, Chestnut, Maple and Elm Street. . . . Could the strumpets from the stews of Corinth, Ephesus or Tarsus fetch a groan or sigh more quickly than the dimpled thighs of lasses from St. Joseph or Topeka?** (*p. 2*)

The earlier process of exorcism and celebration is being repeated —on a new level. Later in the book he recalls sitting in his mother's room in Kansas City, "filled with a fatherless emptiness" (p. 168) and asks further along, "Why was it impossible for me to let go of the misery of my boyhood?" (p. 220). He is able to "let it go" in this book, finally, because of this process of mythicizing. "Mother and father is one flesh," says Hamlet, and Dahlberg leans

33

on Hamlet's logic (one of his chapter headings, ". . . and so, my mother," comes from this speech by Hamlet) to resolve his quest for a past and an identity. His fatherless emptiness is filled in his beautiful and final acceptance of a mother who had been both mother and father.

When the image of her comes up on a sudden—just as my bad demons do—and I see again her dyed henna hair, the eyes dwarfed by the electric lights in the Star Lady Barbershop, and the dear, broken wing of her mouth, and when I regard her wild tatters, I know that not even Solomon in his lilied raiment was so glorious as my mother in her rags. Selah. (*pp. 233–234*).

Dahlberg has accepted the gift and miracle of his life. *Selah,* and *shantih.*

EDWARD KEITH WHITTAKER: *Sorrow and the flea*

> *Geographie without Historie hath life*
> *and motion but at randome, and*
> *unstable. Historie without Geographie*
> *like a dead carcasse hath neither*
> *life nor motion at all.*
> (*Peter Heylyn,* Microcosmus, *1621*)

In discussing *The Flea of Sodom* and *The Sorrows of Priapus,* I
want to focus on the myths Edward Dahlberg has as much manu-
factured as observed; I want to discuss his method, his mytho-
poesis, as well as his matter. Northrop Frye says somewhere that
Blake considered the body was weak enough without its being
separated from the soul, so he tried to unite them to see if he could
hoist man out of his trough to a better Body, visibly a better Soul.
Edward Dahlberg has set himself the same task. Like William
Blake, he will not blink at the process or at his materials. Means
are temporary ends and must be treated accordingly.

The abbreviations of the titles of Dahlberg's works cited at the ends of quota-
tions throughout this article translate as follows:

AFO   *Alms for Oblivion* (with a foreword by Sir Herbert Read), Minneapolis,
        University of Minnesota Press, 1964.
CM   *The Carnal Myth,* New York, Weybright and Talley, 1968.
CTBL   *Can These Bones Live* (with a preface by Sir Herbert Read), Ann Arbor,
        University of Michigan Press, 1967.
EDR   *The Edward Dahlberg Reader* (edited and with an Introduction by Paul
        Carroll), New York, New Directions, 1967.
EOOT   *Epitaphs of Our Times,* New York, George Braziller, 1967.
FS   *The Flea of Sodom* (with a foreword by Sir Herbert Read), Norfolk,
        Connecticut, New Directions, 1950.
LA   *The Leafless American* (edited and with an Introduction by Harold
        Billings), Sausalito, Roger Beacham, 1967.
RH   *Reasons of the Heart,* New York, Horizon, 1965.
SP   *The Sorrows of Priapus,* Norfolk, New Directions, 1957.

The first part of *The Sorrows of Priapus* limns the faculties of "civilized" man, sorry by comparison to those of other mammals, creeping things and "savages." He does not fare well; indeed, Dahlberg considers that "He is an intermediate form; the highest man will have no scrotum; it is ludicrous for a moral philosopher to scrape and scratch as any worm" (*SP,* pp. 53–54). Dahlberg's Man is recognizable, even in his misery. Dahlberg does not find him potent enough to deserve some national identification, like Aeneas, Adam, Albion, or the Green Man. Priapus, that garden god, is everywhere the same and ludicrous, Dahlberg says, and proves his claim.

The phallus has always been considered an unkempt beast. Though matrons and virgins brought fillets and hyacinths to this rude, homely god, it was never his face, but rather his abilities that were worshipped. . . . Nearly every ancient idol was priapic. This was the god that protected the garden and seed-time, and who was associated with the melon, the leek, and the apples of Haran which were aphrodisiacs.

(*SP,* pp. 27–28)

Primitive numbering is sometimes done this way: "1—2—3—heap." Except for obvious comparisons of the sizes of heaps, large numbers are not differentiated. Dahlberg's paragraphs work so. They do not always progress lineally but are instead semiassociative. His style is therefore a sort of middle way between drama and storytelling or exposition.

In *Edward Dahlberg: American Ishmael of Letters,* there is an essay by Joseph Slate which contains valuable insight into the technique of *The Sorrows of Priapus.* He notes that Dahlberg achieves his effects by the use of irony and the apothegm. The double nature of Priapus/forgetful man is explored in many ways: Dahlberg employs parallelism; he varies his mode of diction from clause to clause; he twists his syntax ("Ham and Cush were the original artists, for painting is all about the nudity of other people and ourselves"). Slate says of Dahlberg's style:

Each sentence stands alone. The lack of connection by pronouns is significant. The paragraph is a collection of separate sentences, not a logically related unit. This discontinuity not only demands of the reader an unusual capacity for seeing unity where it is not apparent ("a book for brave readers

and poets," Dahlberg calls *The Sorrows*), but it also turns the reader back to a time when the bestiary was a primordial list, a creative ritual, and very close to myth.

(p. 181)

Dahlberg's view of the world is that it is composed of ever-lastingly discrete particles whose purpose is at least to try to come together. His style is perhaps the most apt vehicle for rendering the indecisiveness of his Man, who is at odds with himself and yet who, because Dahlberg refers to him continually *as man,* is constant in his sorrow, knowing not which way to turn and unable to keep himself from turning.

Man has not always been so intelligent.

> **Men were plant and cowries of the shore,**
> **Woman a potherb, her legs and hair were rain.**

(*LA,* p. 82)

We have small evidence of primeval lewdness, says Dahlberg; civilization is the kingdom of infamy. Man is no longer a giant or amoral. "Jared, Mahalalel and Methuselah begat without the assistance of the female, and these immense mastodons had no minds or privy organs, or any knowledge of their uses" (*SP,* p. 51).

Thought is death and the Fall was into sexual guilt and the swamp of self-consciousness, that trifling awareness we have of the various knobs and hollows of our dithering bodies.

The ears of Aphrodite are small, rotund and toothsome, but the lobes of the male are a wallet into which he stuffs his greed, gossip and carnal stupidity. Ears, often no better than the sow's, have a sluttish aspect; they root on the sides of the head, and like the pig can be fed mire and almost any filth.

(*SP,* p. 23)

It is an uproariously bitter joke that man should consider himself the paragon of creation, says Dahlberg. The difference between man and the rest of the universe is that he thinks, and where has this marvelous ability gotten him? ". . . since man is not going to be different for a thousand millenniums he should select certain animals to teach him to be just, eat and gender at regular intervals, and blush" (*SP,* p. 29). Most animals fornicate in one position only. Many do not even face each other. The human animal writes books about the myriad and inflammatory contortions he supposes are suitable for his coupling; they are brags about his accomplishments. His dearest dream is often to be granted one new whiff or glimpse of a human body, "for what man sees arouses him."

Consistency of behavior need not altogether be despised.

A profligate man who suddenly behaves as though he has saintly traits is a scoundrel because he has stolen our eyesight and understanding. Woe to him who has cultivated a vicious man who unexpectedly resolves to be benevolent.

(*RH*, p. 125)

Birds and beasts know almost unerringly when and where to sleep and how to avoid the intemperance of the elements. They are often convivial too, and if they aren't, they know whom to avoid and are often shunned. Those birds who leave their eggs in others' nests try to do so covertly. If a bird is wicked or lewd, he at least obeys the bird law of kind. "The albatross sports with the frigate, the dolphin, and the shark without filling the stomach of one of his companions, and this is a proverb" (*SP*, p. 35). In cities, men live on top of one another and beside themselves, alone.

The solitary loses his ability to be with others for whatever he does is for himself, which is wicked. He becomes very predacious and has a scorn for failure, and his madness for lucre is terrible. He canonizes the thief, the criminal, and simpers at justice, adultery, falsehood and specious scales. His sole aim is itching and going somewhere else, and he has not the least regard for the difference between good and evil.

(*SP*, p. 35)

Men grow degenerate far from river banks and the bulrush, or lose their song or powers without the marine bivalve, but what fowl goes alone? The widgeons fly together, and gabble with one another in pools as they crop grass or fish for crabs.

(*SP*, p. 36)

In Chapter Five of *The Sorrows of Priapus* Edward Dahlberg says that before the earth was with form and void, strange hermaphroditic creatures occupied great misty space and were content. Though they were visionaries, Saint Paul and William Blake agreed that in Christ there is neither man nor woman. "The anthropoid is more luckless and unintelligent than animals, and the remedy for his ills is not progress, going forward, which is always to his grave, but turning backwards" (*SP*, p. 18).

Part Two of *The Sorrows of Priapus* is called "The Myth-Gatherers" and is dedicated to William Carlos Williams, "Whose perception is primordial genius, [and who] writes, in *In the American Grain*, that the conquerors were overcome by the wild, vast weight of the continent" (*SP*, p. 58). The timeless promise of the New Jerusalem sought ignorantly in the Americas by the first European visitors is what Dahlberg, like Williams, Lawrence, Cooper, Thoreau, wishes to see fulfilled. "The first shall be last, and the last shall be first is geologic scripture" (*SP*, p. 59). That the novelty of the Americas entranced the epically energetic discoverers is well known. The lesson we have from them is equally large and simple—the land must teach us, for we cannot teach the land.

The Spanish hidalgo and Portugal adventurer came for riches, but the harvest was often no more than the piñon nut, tanned hides of the woolly cattle of the Platte, or virgin discovery, which, like learning, is tombstone destiny.

(*SP*, p. 62)

In *The Sorrows of Priapus* Dahlberg tells why the great American divorce between man and the land should never have occurred. That savagery was and is rife is no reason to suppose it ever should have been and shall be. It is necessary that the madness in us and in our soil be admitted before it can be cured.

The American intellect is a placeless hunter. It is a negative faculty which devours rather than quiets the heart. Dakotah is an Indian word for friend though it is a cruel tribe. This is a battle and prairie mind. Its deity is not Christ, but *Quetzalcoatl*, who is wind and snake; and its travail is as fierce as that of the Indian woman who cannot bring forth until she is given the blood of the serpent.

(*SP*, p. 66)

When we look at the remains of the Indian civilizations of rough Central and South America we wonder at their sophistication in the face of the jungle. The Indians possessed no domestic animals, though they had the knack of the wheel. They were excellent astronomers and architects. Giving homage to the land, they were allowed by it to flourish and, as William Carlos Williams writes of exemplary Tenochtitlan, in *In the American Grain:*

> Streets, public squares, markets, temples, palaces, the city spread its dark life upon the earth of a new world, rooted there, sensitive to its richest beauty, but so completely removed from those foreign contacts which harden and protect, that at the very breath of conquest it perished. The whole world of its unique associations sank back into the ground to be reënkindled, never. Never, at least, save in spirit; a spirit mysterious, constructive, independent, puissant with natural wealth; light, if it may be, as feathers; a spirit lost in that soil.

We assume the Indians came to the Americas from Asia. "The American fable is a table of the seasons, the moons, days and annals of the pilgrimages of tribes" (*SP*, p. 66). In Chapter Ten of *The Sorrows of Priapus,* Dahlberg states that all races are the descendants of the three sons of Noah, who peopled the earth following the Deluge. The Hamites were the first Asians, and the first Greeks came from the loins of Japheth. "Genealogy is a vast myth; the record of man, apart from legend, is stepmother history" (*SP*, p. 88).

> The *Quiché Maya* had a jaguar Genesis, and they had an old Semitic word, Balam, meaning soothsayer; like the progane Balaam, in the *Old Testament,* this Balam was the jaguar priest. . . . The *Quiché Maya* say that primeval man was shaped out of mud; Adam in Hebrew was virgin red clay. . . . The Adam of the Quiché was unable to move his head, and his face fell to one side, and he could not look behind, which is the tragedy of the inhabitants of the New World. He had no mind, which is nothing but turning one's eyes toward the past.
>
> (*SP*, p. 88)

Much lore was lost in those first anabases, and both Dahlberg and Williams realize that in America the land has always been man's dictator. Dahlberg claims further that

> Our fate has been so far from heroic because we no longer push back all limits and horizons as the discoverers did. There is enormous metaphysics in the lives of Cartier, Pigafetta, Behaim. For this reason one cannot reject as evil a Cortes or a De Soto; even their cruelties are Homeric, and I know when saying this that I am falling into the greatest danger of our times, our concern with aesthetics, which is the avoidance of human and moral judgments.
>
> (*EOOT*, p. 124)

40

That statement aligns Dahlberg momentarily with Williams and Olson; the various European priests and plunderers and the Indians and the *Continent* are the raw material with which the American annalist has to work. Unlike the other two writers, Dahlberg desires the transfer of the pieties of the Old World to mellow the savagery of the New.

The first Spaniards, Portuguese, French, and English found little recognizable in all *terra damnata* save their own rapacity, and they comprehended that seldom enough. "There was no Virgil or Propertius to lament the feral peccary, tapir, armadillo, condor, or guanoco" (*SP*, p. 101).

The legends of a continent without household animals, timorous streams, and social birds, except the macaw and parrot bred in the swamps of the Sertão, are battle Kabalah of creation. It is told that after the Deluge the coyote planted the feathers of the various birds from which sprang up all the tribes of men.

(*SP*, p. 104)

Many notable Indian tribes were spawn of water or land-weakened water and this accounts for their "grum honesty" and several hardinesses. The epic significance or potency of a region has nothing to do with its small size, for the streams of Palestine and the island-dotted pond between the Peloponnese and Asia Minor occasioned the Psalmist, the Prophets, and Homer. Contemplation and utterance are possible beside the little waters but "Large, feral waters confound the races of the earth" (*SP*, p. 107).

The wafted American must look at, listen to, travel upon his great rivers, his endless humped and bowled land—in the flesh and in the imagination—to approximate himself to their secrets he does not now understand. Only then will he see that all rivers are one and only then will he begin to inherit what Edward Dahlberg calls his "native agony." Dahlberg summarizes the early assaults on the Mississippi by La Salle, whom he uses to prove one of his axioms about human nature—character is fate, or we do what we are.

La Salle had a February genius; he was a cold cosmographer, having fewer vices to moult than Cortes and De Soto. The Cavalier had little of earth, air, fire. . . . It is doubtful that he ever found the source of the

41

Mechasipi, which is warm and falls into the Gulf, because character, free will and destiny are the same. La Salle chose Canada, and North America, a Golgotha's vineyard, as his water and burial site.

(SP, p. 112)

La Salle was a driven man and the harshness of his struggles set the teeth on edge. In a winter before they went southward La Salle's men were forced to live off the land. They rooted beneath the snow for acorns like the starving deer. La Salle explored a territory as large as that of the sons of Shem; he was a greater geographer than Menelaus, who voyaged to Joppa. What was his hero's portion? Returning to New France, the Governor, he found himself unfavored. He shuttled between France, Frontenac, and his river, created no colonies, discovered vast waters and a few Indians, and was dispatched in the bush by a mutineer.

The severest deity is need, a god who confers benefits upon who toil with chance. . . . Memory is our day of water tutored by want. . . . Water is death but man must seek it. All our seeming wakings are the debris of evening waters; most dreams come from mean shallows, and are the digestive rot of secure bottoms; prophecies rise up from the marine depths ancient as the Flood. We are cartographers, unheeding the singing maggots, or bereft of the Angel.

(SP, p. 114)

Finally, the soil; the American, says Dahlberg, needs to open his eyes and to take his shoes off. "Forest is the hope of the disciples; more learned than the fig is wildest ground" (SP, p. 117)— WHICH DOES NOT MEAN THAT THEIR NATURES WILL BE SEEN TO BE THE SAME!

Every country contains the minerals of Paradise or is the barren ground for rough annals. Art without austere emasculates the American. . . . The bark of the aspen and birch is the food of the beaver; these are Laconian arts and meals. . . . Canaan was fathoming the limestone strata of the Saskatchewan fringed with purple dogwood and dwarf birch, and populated by the pelican and the brown fishing eagle.

(SP, pp. 117–118)

Edward Dahlberg wrote *The Sorrows of Priapus* first to wake up man to the fact that no wisdom hangs below his belt; and, secondly, to show our continents' man just what his sleepwalking has done for him and what *in this place* he must start to do to avoid further ruination of it and of himself. South America could be

"Ariel," as Dahlberg asserts; imagine and create as an Israel the orchards of cocoa in the pampas and the American Testament will follow soon. Our north is the harsh instructor; taiga and tundra are metaphysicians and admonish frugality and humility. (There are no accidents. The Jesuits, who bared New France, were founded by the soldier-saint Ignatius Loyola. Dahlberg never flags in his approval of Ignatius' educational maxim, "The pupil should be a corpse in the hands of a teacher.") The lonely American is now dying and will not revive unless he turns to his teachers for his lesson. "Where are the little hills which shall bring justice, or the fruits of Lebanon? O forest spectre, ferns, lichen, boleti contain Eden. Be primordial or decay" (*SP*, p. 119).

There is a viable thematic connection between *The Sorrows of Priapus* and *The Flea of Sodom*. In Part One of the former we are shown Man, who is all too human; in Part Two, the effect of the (American) land on him, to the extent that it becomes, practically, his First Cause. In *The Flea of Sodom* (which immediately precedes *The Sorrows of Priapus* chronologically in the Dahlberg canon, being published in 1950, seven years before it), Dahlberg begins by excoriating the follies of his own contemporaries—and, perhaps not yet having pierced to the heart of the American matter, draws his teachings *for* today/what's unknown and unknowing, (primarily) *from* the European headland, stretching East/known.

There are two critical asides in Dahlberg's letters to Isabella Gardner and Stanley Burnshaw which I want to quote before proceeding to write about *The Flea of Sodom*.

. . . is it possible for Homer, Lucian, and Virgil not to dilate the spirit? You must find the source for yourself, not directly in private experience; it is curious that though one has felt acutely, and that all, as Keats says, presses down on one's identity, the approach to his woe and travail is through ritual and myth. One has to tread lightly upon one's veins or blast them into a great darkness. Art is not straight and plain; were it so, then all that is chaff on the palate could easily be translated into Golgotha or the Cana marriage wine. Quicksilver is most useful in an ass's skin, for everything must in some way be covered if the naked truth is to be found and deeply felt.

(*EDR*, p. 291)

The use [of mythological allusion] heightens the entire vision, takes it out

43

of the Valley of Hinnom, out of drab, particular experience and transforms it into a plural vision, all the experiences of other seers that pulse. . . .

(EOOT, p. 287)

What lasts is the past. Dahlberg's essays and letters are usually less packed than the chapters of *The Flea of Sodom;* in the former the "plural vision" is not so much the primary stylistic concern of the author, and the sentences deal more frequently with the mundane, unfertilized by legend. The essays and letters are more emphatically temporal than *The Flea of Sodom,* which is likely the reason the latter has been out of print for so long.

Much of *The Flea of Sodom* is Dahlberg's quest for his European and Near Eastern roots. If *The Sorrows of Priapus* says to us, "Be primordial or decay," it is to the Old World, some of the time, that we must turn for instruction in primogeniture. The reverend and ancient little lands skirting the Sea of Middle Earth—Palestine, Attica, Phoenicia, Italia—deliver their lore. The narrative sections of the book are applications of that lore to an approximately American situation.

At the beginning of *The Flea of Sodom,* Dahlberg has left a note on its luxurious style:

> **If this little book appears opaque, the reason is easy to know: the line is gnomic, pulsing with Ovid, Livy, Strabo, Suetonius, Herodian, Plutarch, the Book of Enoch, and the Apocalypse of Baruch. The similes themselves are definitions of ancient rituals, which are a bucolic physic for men who feed and gender upon our macadam meadows. . . . The purpose of any author is to be artistically mirthful; for no writer can persuade who cannot entertain. Chaucer observes, "a licorous mouth has a lickerish tail," which is a didactic as well as a jolly line. Though this book has some melancholy matter in it, the author hopes that the sentences are made of that bread and wine, and have that accent of the timbrel, with which Saul ascended the holy mountain.**

(FS, pp. 12–13)

Edward Dahlberg has long resolved to be a "jocose iconoclast" (*LA*, p. 57). James Laughlin published *The Flea of Sodom* in a fortuitous season, and Dahlberg's sketches of radical activists and bohemians in that book are tied superficially to events in the Thirties, but the foolishness and hypocrisy are just as relevant to the quacks of contemporary radicalism, both activist and pacifist. (They reappear, perhaps, much diminished in stature and significance, as Kerouac's *Subterraneans* and as "The Whole Sick Crew" in Thomas Pynchon's *V*.) Dahlberg's caricatures make rubble of time generally because of the style in which they are presented, and specifically because of their hilarious names—Thersites Golem, Andromache Lucy, Thais Colette, Pilate Agenda, Ephraim Bedlam, Ajax Proletcult.

The Sodomites, who are grotesque as well as recognizable, squander their days and nights in fornication, frenetic political or artistic activity, rabble partying, or seamy gossip. Thersites is a rude and humpbacked Marxist Jew sculptor. Andromache Lucy, his sometime wife, is a political Medusa and the community chest; she takes on a man because he is stylish and drops him (herself creating style and destroying it) when she tires of him. Thersites acquires slumming Pilate Agenda as his patron. All the Sodomites vibrate at the prospect of seeing him—an authentick bourgeois! Pilate imports Spanish sponges and cork, which does not hinder the Sodomites from wheedling him into supporting their maggoty radical schemes. Predictably, Pilate tries to seduce Andromache Lucy; after a while, he fails. Ephraim Bedlam is moderately human. He is a vegetarian playwright who stinks. Ajax Proletcult is a classic activist boor who marches for oppressed workers and drops cigarette ash on Pilate's expensive rugs.

The segment of the book inhabited by the Sodomite rout is called "The Flea of Sodom." It is narrated in the first person by a skinless Janus who is the cause of Sodom's itch. He never fails to insist on the virtue of some species of customary behavior. Everyone walks right through him. Because of his solitude and because he is really no better than his associates except in intention, the narrator collapses to jelly whenever he is given a beck or a touch. The action is credible, for the Flea is almost willy-nilly of Sodom as well as in it.

One night Monsieur Golem Patron entered the 7th Avenue rooms with Golem on one arm and a village trull on the other; they had met her at the china-america internationale restaurant or the workmen's lenin ping-pong club. Andromache, studying the cannery and shoe factory proletarian drama with Ephraim Bedlam, was asked to meet Thais Colette. "She wants to join the gutter queue of spongers, dowds and artists," added Monsieur Golem Patron.

(*FS*, pp. 35–36)

Pilate gives a raucous party for the Sodomites. Longing for his bucolic Missouri childhood, the narrator woefully attends. Stroked by Pilate, he reels; when noticed indirectly by Andromache, he faints. "One will take to his heart an Heliogabalus or a Nero rather than be deserted" (*FS*, p. 45). Pilate Agenda falls into disrepute, not because he is a profiteer, but because he tries inopportunely to seduce some demi-rep. The interest the Sodomites had in centering their activities around him suddenly vanishes; the interest they have in each other vanishes equally miraculously.

> When I saw Golem he fled. Running after him I shouted at his coat tails, "Nabal beadle buttocks, occidental cathartic skin, do not primp and tinkle, soft bowels give pity." Admonishing Golem, lurking in a hall, because truth must correct error, I said, "All the sputum you have given for Madrid will not cure the stinking Bethesda pool of your own spirit. Do you slaver when you see people?" Pushing me away he hurried down the street.
>
> (*FS*, p. 49)

All the Sodomites now derive strength to banish their own boredom as they shun the narrator, who claims to be trying desperately "to relinquish the world for a proverb and lose my reason for the allegory" (*FS*, p. 52). Pilate appears to have come through, to have done just this; but when he attempts to perpetrate a Last Supper on the Sodomites, they hoot at his hypocritical inversion and desert him anew.

> Pilate made a low obeisance and whispered so that not all heard, "Forgive me, if I wash you," which made Golem lift up his voice, "If Pilate says, 'I love man,' look out. If he tells you, 'I know nothing,' beware. But when he speaks low out of the heart, 'I am humble,' run for your life." . . .
> When all had left Pilate I thought, "can the eyes drop water, when the bowels remain a sherd."
>
> (*FS*, pp. 55–56)

At the story's end the Lazarus narrator is desolated by the lack of reverence all around him. What is worse is that this desolation exists inside him—he simply *cannot* leave the nonsensical Sodomites although he knows their souls are leprous. "Going away, I turned back, hungering as Lot's wife did for the lascivious hearths of Sodom" (*FS*, p. 56). Like other Dahlberg heroes at the end of their stories, he is totally raveled, a man only of inanitioned parts. He does not know what to do or how to do it.

> Perhaps I would go to Los Angeles, which is the orchard of Gomorrah,

and not the fig of Israel. I knew I had slain my blood, for Abel was crying out of my veins. What should I do? "Sit," whispered my heart, entreating, "Will ye go away?" to which my soul and flesh replied, "Lord, to whom shall we go?"

(FS, p. 57)

To continue, let us first go back. The opening few pages of *The Flea of Sodom* are a marvelous way for Dahlberg to speak after having published no books for nine years.

> Let us admit, going over the Atlantic was a tragic mistake, and that he who drinks the vile, oceanic froth of Cerberus loses his memory and goes mad. . . . It is better to be slain by a bow of cornel wood or face a warrior in a helmet made of the rind torn from the cork tree than perish by metal. The weapons by which man dies reveal whether he lived with the roe and hind close by the founts of Helicon or in Boreal, gloomy towns.

(FS, p. 15)

The marine exodus, again amnesia, is to Dahlberg a symptom of the sin of sloth. He who possessed his soul within the Pillars forgets it beyond them. "This Atlantic nonentity, muttering Babel's homogeneous words, hatches his slovenly cities anywhere" (*FS*, p. 17). The narrator of the Sodomites' tale takes the general perversity to himself. He would be mythic, returning to "the pruning-hook and Boaz's granary floor" but is instead rational/fallen, lonely and given to loathing himself and all else.

In *The Flea of Sodom* there is a rough pattern: two chapters of narrative in which a prophet without honor tries and fails to cleanse the doors of someone's perception alternate with two chapters in which all characters are subsumed by the vision of Edward Dahlberg, the spirit of that Time he smiths into space for the readers of the book. Chapter Two of *The Flea of Sodom* is called "The Rational Tree," the Eden Tree whose juicy fruit we still covet.

> In Eden there are two trees: "Behold, I have set before thy face life and death, good and evil; choose life." Every Prophet has perished, for if man eat of the Tree of Knowledge he will die, and the Angel with the flaming sword that guards the Tree of Life can never be overcome until men are a different shape, substance, and mind.

(FS, p. 55)

The Rational Tree is the parody of the tree mentioned in the epigraph to Chapter Two of *The Flea of Sodom,* which epigraph

Dahlberg takes from Christopher Smart's *Song to David:* "While Israel sits beneath his fig." The simplicity and singleness of spirit implied by this phrase are the ideals to which the chapter aspires.

What facilitates them? Dahlberg's first notice is that in a simpler past, just measures for all things were sacred. "In . . . Attica the idols stood guard over the market. . . . Job puts his integrity, Archilochus his Iambic, and Shakespeare his Sonnet, in the Balance" (*FS,* p. 61). The gods saw to appropriate prices and recipes, and the cities and people who feared them throve. The ancient city was sane, says Dahlberg, when one knew where to look for what one desired. ". . . in Jerusalem there were separate gates for sheep and asses and camels. . . . Nehemiah tried to restore Zion by repairing the gates for herds and the dung!" (*FS,* p. 63). "What need has man to go beyond the sheepcote, the threshing-floor, and the augur's timbrel? A mortar and a pestle are enough for a culture!" (*FS,* p. 66).

Perhaps if we were not so intent on progress (the avoidance of difficulty), we would not be so cast down by what difficulties we have to face. For example, our smallest diseases are a cause for frenzy; violence is our pornography and death our new obscenity. Job sat to pull at his boils with a piece of cooked mud. Disease was not prevalent among the Israelites when they were decorous and properly energetic.

Removal from simplicity is the inception of the rational mind. There is a difference, finally, between philosophies of legend and metaphysics, the difference of the easing Human Form.

Reason that does not suckle on proverbs and racial images, which are the vine in the blood, bears the grapes of Sodom. . . . 'Let me place my speech in thee,' recites the father, delivering tradition to the Son in the Upanishads. . . .

Mephistophilus promises Dr. Faustus Helen, but he will not cocker his arrogance by talking to him about unhallowed first causes. 'Tell me, who made the world?' cajoles Faustus. 'I will not tell thee,' answers Mephistophilus.

Empedokles rests in Asphodels for putting the Ass's Bladders in the hills to catch the Etesian gales; Speusippus, inventor of the Twig Basket, frolics with the sea-trulls of Neptune who found the vetch. But Anaximander is in Tartarus tethered to his maps, clocks and gnomon. Who would hesitate to be Virgil or Chaucer rather than Aristotle or Plotinos? Proteus's shells smite

the mind more sweetly than Anaxagoras's kosmos, and the Vedic heifer yields more than Plato's philosophy.

(*FS*, pp. 86–87)

Dahlberg is amazed that often he who angrily breaks an idol, which may be salutary, is himself no health for the wound he has created by his destruction.

Diogenes leaves to the vulnerable imagination his malodorous cloak and the raw polypus he ate and from which he died. Cato's last act, the fraying of his entrails, after he read Plato's *The Immortality of the Soul*, punishes mortal mind as much as Socrates, pleasurably scratching his manacled shanks, as he prepares himself for the Hemlock.

(*FS*, pp. 90–91)

Karl Marx swore that the world would remember his carbuncles.

When Edward Dahlberg talks about the dreams of scientific humanists, his words would scorch their ears. A true conservative, he believes there is enough wisdom presently available in the world. Progress, an abstraction, looks ahead. "Evil and Spoiling are in the imagination of families and races" (*FS*, p. 66).

No one can invent a sane habit or one good deity. Man guesses, and comes to judgments after a study of saws and gnomes. 'What has most weight and wisdom pierces the ear.' Pastoral cities and theogonies are not premeditated; they just happen.

(*FS*, p. 90)

Whoever desires to restore Ilium or build an Arcadia is impious and insane. Heraclitus rebuked Homer for attempting 'bring about the downfall of the universe' by removing strife from the world. 'The sun will not overstep his measures; if he does, Erynes, the hand-maids of Justice, will find him out.'

(*FS*, p. 91)

Dahlberg does not advocate giving up the human struggle, however. He believes man's greatest enemy is his own person, not someone else. The Mental Fight is what is worth winning. What gives his arguments cogency is not only the style in which Dahlberg delivers them, but also the fact that for the sake of the Word, Dahlberg himself has lived much of his life unwillingly in the company of the cockroaches and skinny rodents of poverty.

The false and temporizing prophet would abstract not only danger, but also grace and vivacity from the world, in the name of ease. "Time is Caesar's," says Edward Dahlberg, "and those who

49

dwell in it can never discern the Paradise promised by the Angel of the Apocalypse" (*FS,* pp. 93–94). Sin is Babel or "the appetite for a universal ratiocinative Gomorrah where Ahab and Elijah, the Prophet's mantle and Nero's sacred beard, are of the same moral weight, and man and woman, wearing the clothes of sodomy, act as a single sex" (*FS,* p. 95).

Part Three of *The Flea of Sodom* is "The Wheel of Sheol," the vision offered to a fool. Beliar has the chance to avoid ravaging Abel, his ancestry and feeling. Seven prophets create before him a fantastic reflective beast that is man, cow, and horse. They don't do it overtly for his benefit—he's just lucky to be there. The prophets study adages written upon clods while Beliar works the ground for precious metals and gets piles for his efforts. A deep gully separates Beliar's asphalt world from where the "cattle of Elohim" and the seven prophets sit. An olive tree stands on the imaginative side of the gully and beneath it is Wisdom, at whom the loving prophets do not gaze. ". . . All knowledge that is for the living God is in the rear of remembrance, and as the face of God is tomorrow, no man may look at it" (*FS,* p. 101). Rational Beliar faces Wisdom and lusts after her.

Beliar saw the wheels of Elisha's burning chariot, and the starry rings beneath Charles' Wagon loaded with holy censers in which were deposited prayers given as alms by humble penitents. . . . Beliar stole the Wheels and hurried away into the earth with them, and lasciviously shaking before his furnace and stithy, he riveted iron bands around the Wheels, and then commanded them, saying, 'O Wheels, go, go' and these terrible rings of iron went through the whole world.

(*FS,* p. 103)

From that time all knowledge in the world was infected, and strife and lassitude came among people, and pests tore at life everywhere, as life enjoyed the perversion of dying. Beliar is most pitiable, cloaked as a searcher after truth; indeed, he is Faustus. If he lives, it is to forge a graven image of Pandemonium. When he dies, he is more alone than he need be. Time's touch at Beliar's hem makes him conscious that virtue has left him. He seeks an old prophet, ostensibly to learn rest. "The seer . . . resembled an earthen pitcher of old wine" (*FS,* p. 109). Here are Dahlberg's words in the mouth of the prophet:

'Spleen is a sickness, for after a man has loosed his bile, he must walk in the valley of Kidron for a year to be quiet again. Three things you should heed and do: return to the world, but as a timorous stranger with a proverb in his mouth; second, be as nimble as a gazelle to run to a proverb, and as fierce as a lion to devour its meaning; and third, know that forgetting is the depravity of sloth.'

(*FS*, p. 110)

The climax of the tragedy is inevitable and immediate—Beliar realizes that the prophet too is flesh, which is grass. He smirks, and the prophet stifles his anger. Beliar returns to his blacktop world and his devils are worse than ever.

"Bellerophon" is the title of the Fourth Part of *The Flea of Sodom*. "Bellerophon is Odysseus the artist" (*FS*, p. 113), who took and bridled calm Pegasus, slew the Chimaera, was beloved of men, and who proceeded to eat his heart out in solitude because at last, thrown by his mount, he could not assail Olympus. Dahlberg holds the watery artist responsible for his own time, and it is fitting that the artist learn his limits. "No one is on guard enough against his nature, for each man is dear to himself, and thoroughly unprepared for his vices. It is sin to believe in one's character" . . . (*FS*, p. 116). Man (and especially man writing), the difference between brute and God, is mind leavened by "MORTAL TOUCH." With mind alone, man is a machine and the heavens are not pleased by him.

. . . writing, like dying, is a private act, the ritual of the soul in its descent to Styx and the Dream. It is the dying for new forms, the expiratory pang of Orpheus for Eurydice in Hades. The Orphic poet must return as quickly as he can to sane, dry light, for though the Dream writes everything, it is the NEGATIVE ANGEL of the LIVING WILL. Space, shoreless, inward God, and the surging, evening images of Pathless Dream, produce in men, whose will has been relaxed by watery Tartarus, jibing, OWL'D ANGELS of Reason.

(*FS*, p. 114)

These words explain Dahlberg's quarrels with so many writers. Writers are human, and fall from the tightrope between health and madness sometimes—we all walk it, many of us none too well. Dahlberg has a stake driven deep into the ancient psychology of the four elements—earth, air, fire, and water—and often uses them to account, in his criticism, for a writer's personality and his works. In his essay on Herman Melville, Dahlberg writes that "Melville imagined he had taken the paschal lamb of Christ and covered it with the coat of Leviathan. He cringed when he thought of the 'universal cannibalism of the ocean, or unverdured seas'—yet most of his volumes are salt-water folios. A hydromaniac, there was very much more of liquid properties than flesh in his prose style" (*AFO,* p. 124).

In his diatribes against reason in art and politics, in *Can These Bones Live,* Dahlberg mentions further that Melville was a preternaturally lonely man. His objections to James Joyce's *Ulysses* are that it drumbles and that its hero, like Melville's Ishmael, is a disciple of Onan. D. H. Lawrence, whom Dahlberg knew and loved, thought *Ulysses* bad art because it was too rigid and rational.

At times, art does not stand beside life; part of the shaping will loses Life. Whitman made of the body a *res publica,* a public thing; he equated it with "These States," and in so abstracting it, Dahlberg notes, he killed chances for moving belief in its finite and fleshly joys and woes. Whitman is another of Dahlberg's mermen. What is to be done?

The mind, in which the valley and the apples have failed, is depraved, but its negations, provided the Lamb yet lives, gladden the lilies. No knowledge rightly understood can deprive us of the mirth of flowers.

. . . Return to the Fig-trees beneath the walls of Ilium to chant to the timorous, dove-winged mind. Go low, Bellerophon, come down, O learned Dust, Wisdom is our PRAYER. (*FS,* p. 117)

The vigorous end of *The Flea of Sodom* is a cluster of three parables. Their detailed explication is the coda to this essay.

The first parable is the conflict in the speaker's soul over the death of Inspiration, energy, origins, kin, and friends. The Stranger/Doubt/Satan/any accuser, personified, who accosts the "I" of the parable, has "lips whose works have perished" (*FS,* p. 121). Jesus said, "There is nothing from without a man, that entering into him can defile him: but the things which come out of him, those are they that defile the man" (Mark 7:14).

The Stranger in the parable is utterly foreign to its narrator, who resists him throughout with growing strength. This consolidation of error is akin to Jesus' temptation in the wilderness. The Devil we have with us always we must force to declare himself. The joy or "the doves and turtles" the Stranger comes to abduct are the slight and innocent pleasures we need in our essential solitude. Their possession is grounds for Accusation. The narrator's reply to the Stranger is Quixotic, the reply of all faith to all doubt, vanquishing it if only for a season—"The birds are hurt, and the branches have slept [in all honesty he is forced to admit that the world is not perfect, though he also notes its virtue], but the grass leaps up, and no one sees its Prophetic Increase" (*FS*, p. 121).

But why admit anything? If it's true, whose fault is that? Admissions are just what the Stranger wants; though he departs, the door is open for his return. The narrator puts his time to good use —"I washed my truths in nitre," he says; I cleansed the gates of my perceptions, the objects of which are pastoral. One is most vulnerable when rejoicing is possible. God is subtle, but the Devil is malicious. "Prove yourself" is his reasoner's curse, trying to blight the furrows, flowers, and sweet waters the narrator has been tending. Contact with these decent products—"Experience is in the fingers," said Thoreau—or better, LOVE, enables the narrator (or anybody who combines instead of sundering) to reply mildly to the Stranger, even when slammed by him. The Vine grows; the error has been detected and rebuked. If Winter is upon us, we know where Spring lies waiting to be awakened.

At the end of *Because I Was Flesh,* Dahlberg writes that his mother, dead, is and is not. Corpses have sentience, says *The Carnal Myth.* What movement there is in gray Sheol, "the Wind blowing in the Griefless Cliffs" (*FS*, p. 121) cannot be enabled further by him who yet lives ("the Growing Vine"). The Vine grows, however, despite limitations set upon its nourishing faculty.

The second parable is an exercise in self-knowledge. In *Can These Bones Live* (p. 53), Dahlberg thunders, "Enough of this man is split, that poet is mad, and that novelist is class-conscious. What need had the artist to make himself whole, were he not split?" The "I" in the second parable looks at his desires, and finds—at least he's honest—his actions. "When I cried, 'Let the Ground abhore me, if I go Proud,' I saw me lipping my knowledge" (*FS*, p. 122). Who can afford to rebuke another, to neglect his duty, even for an instant? Duty is the placing of others before self. The winnowing of good from evil is the only hygiene.

The Crags and Mountain Stone, that saw the Ewes bleeding in the cote from the Tiger's Tooth, are humble, praying hills; God and Christ Praise the TIGER'S TOOTH.

(FS, p. 122)

That is the paradox and struggle of trying to be "the Whole Body and Intelligence" (*EOOT,* p. 279), the agony of ART, or Living with impurity. That crag and mountain are humble and pray is hard to see, but good to hope for, and work toward. That God and Christ praise the TIGER'S TOOTH is easy to see for a cynic, hard to take for an idealist. "Fathers of Isaacs, cease dissembling;/ Will every thicket yield a ram?" says the poetess Isabella Gardner.

Perhaps we must be brutal without fondnesses. But why go out of our way to slaughter everything we come across? The second parable is a plea for the recognition of our natures, by us who have to live with them and try to make them better. It is good to know where to begin. We sin well enough without our conscious aid; why accomplish that part of our fate, when it accomplishes us well enough as it is? Although Dahlberg says that "no one goes beyond the boundaries of himself," he also says something more pertinent: "It is hideous and coarse to assume we can do something for others and absolutely vile not to attempt to do it."

In Parable III are echoes of Beliar's encounter with the decorous prophet. A Delicate Man approaches the narrator, asking advice in crisis. ". . . Shall I . . . seek Gabriel by Chebar to be mocked?" (*FS,* p. 123). He dangles the bait of one seeming to need solace, and is answered with what might be Promethean advice—"Sow anger and bitter leaves by quiet waters" (*FS,* p. 123). "Without Contraries is no Progression," said Blake. As in the second parable, the advice of the wise is to *try* to separate good from evil. Dahlberg also says (in *The Carnal Myth,* I think, and elsewhere), "God bless the sharper"; dupe and sharper *are.* It is better to be the former than the latter. "Nobody has a choice, but if he does not take it, he is a poltroon" (*CM,* p. 4). The prophet also gives quietist advice:

'. . . say to TOPETH, SIGH; trouble no leaf or fallow, and fear most the knowledge of the evening wolves. Go aside, when the Willows open, and

wait for the Wren's feet that press upon the throat to part the mouth for the little, pained words, the small Wren words, the soft, hurt moods of birds treading warm waters.'

(FS, p. 123)

He wishes to tell the Delicate Man what the stinking Lazarus narrator told Golem earlier in the book: "soft bowels give pity." Such compassion is the mood required for the growth of the spirit. We need the Grapes, *more* than it is necessary to ransack the winepress for the detritus that accompanies them. While Sir Herbert Read was alive, Dahlberg continually hounded him to affirm his faith in the great writers and thinkers of the past instead of wasting any time in frets at the ephemeral lice thriving in the armpit culture of the present.

Unfortunately, the Delicate Man is not ripe for good advice, and tries to destroy the narrator-prophet with a sly phrase. In the narrator's last sentence, the book's end, Dahlberg again employs the device of the "I" addressing itself: "O my Bitterness, I am the SHAME Crying out of the Ground" (*FS,* p. 123). Such a conclusion may not seem spectacular, but it must be recalled that the whole of *The Flea of Sodom* (whose physical dimensions are about 4"x6"x½") is devoted to concision. Eternity is in the palm of the hand. The parables are records of tiny internal conversations; the lessons Dahlberg seeks to learn and to teach are those of convention rightly understood, the simplicity of the everyday heaven in the wise infancy of our civilization's annals.

One of Blake's hellish proverbs asserts, "Truth can never be told so as to be understood and not be believed." This is a worthy adage, and should serve as epigraph to some of the volumes of woe and harangue about our present inability to act with any grace after we have taken what we think is thought.

The conclusion to Parable III of Edward Dahlberg's *The Flea of Sodom* must be seen in connection with everything beyond it, as must the wound received by the prophet just previously, which caused his anguished affirmation. The lucid and heroic "yea" is what must be spoken while police and demonstrators devour each other and the lights go out in the windows of the chaste and the lewd alike.

RAYMOND ROSENTHAL: *The carnal myth*

That Edward Dahlberg is one of America's most important writers is becoming clearer with every book he writes and publishes. But what is his cause? It is interesting to note that the critics, although almost uniformly laudatory, are not quite sure of its limits and lineaments. Allen Tate, for example, locates Dahlberg's *mystique* in his opposition to the state, and connects him with that line of American loners that runs from Thoreau to Randolph Bourne; he is "the poet as the perpetual dissenter and outcast. Dante was exiled from his city, with a price on his head; but what had brought this upon him he accepted in principle since he could not have entertained a theory which would justify resistance *as such* to the City." On the other hand, Herbert Read hails him as "our twentieth-century Thoreau, seeking the understanding of the past which will be the understanding of our land and ourselves. . . . His career demonstrates that there is no tradition for American writers: 'We are the eternal infant aboriginals,' as he has said, and each artist must take the journey into the backwoods alone if he is to reach the plateau of achievement where Edward Dahlberg stands."

I have read *The Carnal Myth* six times, and I now feel confident that I understand its main outlines sufficiently well to write a review of the book. Dahlberg's cause, his importance lie in his ingrained suspicion of the rationalistic, scientific heritage which has imprisoned intellect in our time. He knows, instinctively—and this is the virtue and defect of his auto-didactic limitations—that above reason and the soul or spirit stands what Dante called *"il ben dello intelletto,"* that is, the good of the intellect, that light of wisdom which is perpetual source of interpretation and transformation. Dahlberg intuitively knows that the method of this form of intellect is the explanation of myths, the presentation of symbols, the search for ancient wisdom. And this is precisely the form taken by *The Carnal Myth,* which Joseph Evans Slate, one of the contributors to Mr. Billings' interesting volume, describes as a "bestiary . . . or moral book of erotic beasts . . . [whose] scope is encyclopedic and its retrospective movement embraces the entire history of living matter."

Dahlberg is famous or infamous—depending on the degree of the critic's tolerance for heretical opinion—for his attacks on modern literature. Yet his book *The Carnal Myth* is a magnificent example of the montage method used with a brilliance that the self-proclaimed modernists might reflect on with advantage. It is precisely the tension between his love and veneration for the wisdom of the past and his battered, reluctant immersion in the present that imparts a note of conflict and longing to these queer, astonishingly evocative mosaics of quotation, garnered and set out on the page with an originality that pedestrian scholarship could never achieve. In this sense, he is a true modern, like Eliot, Valéry, and Joyce. He cannot settle down comfortably in an uncomfortable epoch; tradition is not a lifeless institution for him but rather the reminder of tragedy that goads him to feats of incomparable juxtaposition and analogy.

Self-revelation is a heavy Petrine doubt hanging about my neck. That is what writing is. I fume away my gloom and imagine I am gaining a knowledge of my nature, and that is sufficient to make a Goya cower.

Only a writer steeped in the classical awareness of human limitation could make the illuminating parallel between the terrible trials and hardships of the Spanish conquistadors in America and the sexual gluttony described and excoriated by the classics. "Who can muse," he says in his preface, "upon the disasters of Panphilo de Narvaez or the pilgrimage of Cabeza de Vaca, who walked naked from the Atlantic to the Rio de las Palmas (the Rio Grande), without understanding that suffering is the Buddha of all flesh?" And his musings have given us perhaps the most profound scrutiny of America's rapacious beginnings—its indigenous identity—to be found in our literature. Acknowledging his debt to that other, first explorer of the American past, William Carlos Williams, "the only poet with the historian's faculty of the American earth," Dahlberg plunges deeper and further by linking all these frightful assaults on the virgin wilderness with an ancient warning that was being flouted and ignored.

The Quiché Maya papyri are jaguar psalms. Aztec hieroglyphs are water demons and the human skulls sacrificed in the oratories. Thoreau is a wild quaggy testament; the strongest books of the American smell of the slime, the horny spicules of sponges, and the spermaceti of leviathan.

Dahlberg's true rebelliousness can be traced directly to his fierce reverence for the past. "The writer's occupation," he proclaims, "according to Ben Jonson, is a 'sacrament of misery.' To be truthful is to dwell in a tomb described as society."

The difficulty of interpreting Dahlberg can be located in the fact that here he is a religious writer without a religion, or rather in search of one. Myth, for many, would seem to be an empty literary exercise, an ornamentation. Dahlberg is after much greater game. He is doing what D. H. Lawrence said American writers must do if our unfledged continent is ever to find its soul: he is ransacking our primeval past to find the roots of a new religion. He himself is not dure, like all true prophets.

Living in the age of separation, I had a clandestine wish I could not repress: not having written this work to instruct others, I hoped it would be a remedy of sorts for those who are broken, my sole kin, wherever they are. . . . I made apothegms, never failing to be concerned with style first and last, but prayed after they were framed they might be a scanty value to those remote hermits, dying in the Arctic Circle of the literati. Had I the dung of the musk ox as fuel in the frozen regions to warm them?

But anyone who reads *The Carnal Myth* with my warning in mind will come away marvelously refreshed and reawakened. The Indians on our continent lived in mythical symbiosis with that "spirit of place" which, as Lawrence declared and as Dahlberg intimates, must be experienced, lived through, struggled against, and finally reconciled if a land or a country is to grow and flourish. The ghosts that haunt the American land are ancient ghosts that have been transplanted by the spirit and need human and mythical recognition before they can be understood and, perhaps, banished.

58

The western people have sepulchred away the sun and the moon; and the American is far from the Indian god rivers, bays, rain and maize that give him images, without which he is sourceless. Until he is connected with the fens, the ravines, the stars, he is more solitary than any beast. Man is a god, and kin to men, when he is a river, a mountain, a horse, a moon. . . . Hindu writing is meditative, and the domestic heifer is sacred and near the Buddha. The American legend is the mesa and the bison; it is the myth of a tragic terrain stalked by banished men.

Dahlberg's prose is eminently quotable; he is perhaps our most consummate rhetorician, but he also has a great deal to say. His books are worth the trouble of meditation, of rereading, of pondering over again and again. I myself wonder whether he *knows* fully and intimately the profundity of his own wisdom. He is indeed like a seer whose vision sometimes escapes himself; the delight of the imaginative transport blurs the clarity of perception. At times one has the feeling that he believes America can be saved only by an ancient past, that the Indians and their ceremonies and rituals are meaningless to us, that spirituality can only come from elsewhere. He is an aesthete in religion too, and perhaps that is why he mistakes his own wisdom for a lesser thing than it is. The truth is in his rhythms, his eloquence, not in his explanations.

But once it has been said, even in this confused clairvoyant manner, it is quite clear to all. It is true that America has never been redeemed by the spirit, by the *ben dello intelletto*. Dahlberg is important because he points a new way: "Ragged earth seldom produces mild men; the rivers of the New Continent are choleric, and the reason that the rapacious Scamander, with whom Achilles fought, appears to be small and of little importance is that Homer has tamed this stream."

Dahlberg is a lone searcher for the true myths of human destiny in our violent, barren land, for, as he says, "Man is the animal who thinks, but he cannot employ his intellect without losing his reason, which is why Cristobal Colón saw mermaids in the waters near the Antilles, or how Plato conceived the *Timaeus*." From such statements, American criticism, if it were really mythical in orientation, could evolve a new corpus of thought and revelation to counter the materialism and sensationalism growing on all sides.

ANTHONY BURGESS: *Honoring a prophet
in his own country*

The best, said W. B. Yeats, lack all conviction. They also, if they
are writers, lack royalties. It is a truism beloved of the garret-
starvers that talent and material rewards subsist in an inverse
ratio, but it would be dangerous to ignore statistics altogether.
Hemingway was a great writer who became a rich one and, for
that matter, William Shakespeare didn't die poor. But of all contemporary writers in English, Edward Dahlberg best fulfills the
gloomy thesis that genius is its own reward. When we examine the
worth of his books, and after that his sales, we're inclined to come
right out with a Yeatsian scorn directed at the world of literary
commerce. Dahlberg is great, and he is greatly ignored.

Not, however, by the intellectuals (who, alas, account for a
minimal percentage of book sales). Dahlberg was always big
stuff. He was never, however, the right sort of big stuff for the
great American public. There has always been too much of the
tables-of-the-law thumping prophet about him, as well as too much
curious learning. He never indulged in the poster-paint slapping of
Whitman in the last century or of Thomas Wolfe in this, knocking
out huge impressionist canvases to the greater glory of the American Dream. He prefers the past to the future, and ultimately he
withdraws to a hermitage where language is more important than
its referents. This sort of thing is not popular in towns like Zenith.

60

And yet one might have expected Dahlberg's autobiographical novel, *Bottom Dogs,* to be the sort of success that, say, John Dos Passos' *U.S.A.* turned out to be. After all, it was published in 1930, when there was a fair audience of the disillusioned, and when pictures of a downtrodden American proletariat fortified discontent at one end of the scale and provoked guilt at the other—both delicious emotions. But Dahlberg's crime was to distrust the Marxists—"venal and coarse," a gang of political narcissists. He never got on with the moral simplifiers, which is essentially what the political activists are, and he was less concerned with generalizing from his own wretched poverty-stricken beginnings than with setting down—in all its stink and sodor—the precise *quidditas* of that underdog boyhood.

Even Dahlberg's anti-Nazi novel, *Those Who Perish,* refused to condemn from the viewpoint of partisan commitment. And, another obstacle to general acceptance, the book came too soon—in 1934. Another five years were to go before the really profitable cashing-in on the shadow of the swastika began. Still, it is astonishing that *Those Who Perish* should sell only 200 copies. Depending as he does on a publisher's economic, not merely aesthetic faith, no author can hope even to be heard at a whisper's level if he cannot bring the smell of selling potential with his manuscript.

Those 200 copies were a death sentence. Dahlberg was condemned to be put to virtual silence until 1947, when Herbert Read so praised the British edition of *Can These Bones Live* (375 copies in the U.S.) that at least the critics had to take, and go on taking, notice. Yet the laudations, which compared Dahlberg to Nietzsche, Joyce, and Lawrence, could not tempt a wider public.

It is possible to see from one particular book—first published ten years ago—why the public gets so frightened. This is *The Sorrows of Priapus,* which *The Carnal Myth* completes, coming as it does from the same original manuscript. It is an anti-flesh book; it is crammed with evidence of astonishingly wide reading; it is pessimistic; it is unclassifiable. It is, in a word, un-what-America-likes-to-think-American. Here, taken from *The Carnal Myth,* is a gobbet of quintessential Dahlberg:

The white man is a captive of the new continent, according to William Carlos Williams, the only poet with the historian's faculty of the American earth. The beginnings of the American are a Babel to himself. A stranger in the earth, he excludes the sullen weather of New York, which has no dry heat or austere winter. The North American Caliban, neither hot nor cold, cannot attach himself to his neighbor; and solitude is fatal to the affections. The Canadian Indians, after losing their kindred, tore up their tents, destroyed their possessions, and wailed together.

The American has been dwarfed by a continent so vast that it cannot ever be a home; he turns in on himself and becomes perverted. No very popular doctrine. But note the whiff of the archaic, as though Dahlberg were putting on stylized prophetic mantles (sometimes Hellenic, more often Hebraic); note the artful allusion —"fatal to the affections"; "tore up their tents"; note the chiseled effect of every sentence—not a relaxed American voice but a jawbone used as a hammer. You will puzzle as to whom Dahlberg reminds you of, and you will come up with Charles M. Doughty— another desert man who had to build his own painful prose style. After that, you can see in Dahlberg only uniqueness.

I recognize Dahlberg's greatness, but I must confess that I am often repelled by the sense of multiple personae, so that I seem to be observing an act rather than coming into contact with an urgent voice. Dahlberg says: "Should a jobbernowl complain that his jocose tale is tedious, flat, and sodden, I repeat what Robert Burton, fantastical author of *The Anatomy of Melancholy,* hurled at such an abominable fellow: 'If you don't like my book, go and read another.'" Now that "jobbernowl" is too whimsically contrived, like something in Charles Lamb's abominable Elianizings: It is devised for admiration (how Elizabethan, how Rabelaisian he is!); it is a hint that we're in for a verbal *tour de force*. And so we are. Beneath the glitter there's a solid and enduring pessimism —the mark of a writer who thinks so highly of the human potential that he cannot but be let down by the human actuality. But there's plenty of comfort in words, words, words.

Edward Dahlberg has written in *The Sorrows of Priapus* that "each poem or book is Demeter's quest for Persephone, who is the furrow, seed-time and affection, or an act against nature." *Do These Bones Live* is also the sorrowing wisdom of a writer who has lived intimately with prophets, sages, and the myths of the race of men. Dahlberg, in violation and intensity, is reminiscent of Blake, that lone and terrible genius, who had the courage to live by the precepts of wisdom and imagination—and no other. Indeed, Dahlberg is a prophet in our midst, who, as Stanley Kunitz has written, gets the shabby treatment that all prophets receive.

Do These Bones Live is an alembic, a fiery distillment that transmogrifies the good reader and flenses the weak. In fact, it can be read only by good readers, for Dahlberg draws his allusions and maxims from an astonishing variety of sources to wed them in parable and poetic intensity. As a poet he compresses in each phrase intense wisdom, and there is no hiatus in his phrasing or coherency in total structure.

In this work one seeks in vain for the shibboleth canons of contemporary criticism. The author is independent of the academic investment in the *name,* the *cliché;* though he has taught in six universities, he writes with the wisdom of the heart and not with the epicene glyphs of the academies.

The central theme of *Do These Bones Live* is the sad denial of the quest of Persephone, of love everywhere and in literature; above all in literature. Man has been alienated from himself by the loveless rituals of state, church, and economy; man has been alienated by his forgetfulness of the past, by his disavowal of wisdom. Man has been alienated by fear of his own psychic nature, by his denial of the cravings of spirit and flesh, by his fear of touch which is manifested in a superhygienic worshipping of white sterility and its fearsome twin—the explosion of his own caldroned urges; man has alienated himself by the inhuman expression of himself in the forms of contemporary culture.

The book is divided into eight sections, each unified by Dahlberg's vision of man meeting the universe, with his triumphs, failures, the certainties and the mysteries of his quest. In the "Man-Eating Fable," the author weaves a parable drawn from Shakespeare, Homer, Goya, Keats, Sir Thomas Browne, Machiavelli, and the *Gospels* on the anthropophagous nature of man. "Hamlet's tragedy is our horoscope, so much we know; but history does not improve man and auguries do not make him wiser."

In "Thoreau and Walden," Dahlberg extols the "purest parable ever written in America" and affirms that "we do not perceive what we canonize." The pervading insistence of *Do These Bones Live* is that the myth, meaning, purpose, allegory underlying great lives and great works are dulled through the insanity of society; that the transformation of a myth into a man's heart is a spiritual necessity. What we usually achieve, through institutions, is the crippled ideal.

In Part IV, which is the essence of the book, Dahlberg ranges American culture. "There has been no more clinkered land for the artist to live than America." Here are the themes of puritanism, the denial of the flesh, the distortion of our rarest spirits who ultimately are "of the mass." Emily Dickinson, "starving in her father's garden," the grave-worshipping Poe, the "athletically amative Walt Whitman," our critics, "sterile grammarians," our naturalism, "matter in motion loathing itself." He condemns the French strain of realism that has poisoned our writers and has produced scatophagous scribblers, Faulkner, Dos Passos, Dreiser, Hemingway, the "proletarian novelists," the writers who merely mimic and paint as slaves of locality and of mangled perception. The weakness of our writers, unlike the nineteenth-century Russians or Elizabethans, is in creating ikons and images. We have expressed our worst possibilities, so Dahlberg has declared, because we have sacrificed *being* to *locality* and have forgotten our memory. He laments that American literature (and he deplores distinction between American and many other literatures as a violation of time, space, and perception) has been Ezekiel's Valley of Dry Bones.

In "The Bridegroom's Ache," "The Cross and the Windmills," in "Woman, Superstition and Images," Dahlberg reiterates his theme of the persistence of dogma and denial, the continuation of the "dirty paraphernalia of sorrow, horror and belief," the fact that "man exchanges one set of pieties for another but does not thereby become free." The rituals of state and church and man's enslavement by the ikon and anthropophagic fury, he repeats, and man must not be denied his spirit or he will *eat* the whole world. All ages are contemporary; the cannibalistic bloodbath of genocide, fascism, communism are the human sacrifices of antiquity. The exchange of mariolatry for the adoration of Shirley Temple and the sadic antics of Popeye the Sailor are but shifting forms of enslaved perception. "O let man laugh the *gods* out of this world so the heart may live in it."

The ancient Calimachus said that a great book was equivalent to a great evil, but he never explained what he meant. Dahlberg's book is a great book and is equivalent to a great exploration of both good and evil. There is nothing like it in American letters.

KAY BOYLE: *A man in the wilderness*

In a letter written in 1958 from Mallorca, Spain, to William Carlos Williams in Rutherford, New Jersey, Edward Dahlberg cries out in despair: "As soon as you have architecture anywhere today you have foolish opinionated buildings, dogmatic functionalism, and all the depravity of the up-to-date, inhuman city. Nobody is educated enough any more to build a simple, unaffected home which is as good, and has as much feeling, as an ancient proverb. When I look at a motorcycle or a taxi there are tears in my heart. For all the earth is ours, our habitation and sepulcher, and every country that falls under the infamy of money is a terrible wound to every other people."

Writing to Lewis Mumford from Berkeley, California, in 1953, Dahlberg reproaches Mumford for his worship of the machine, and cautions him that to see "beauty in machinery is a great perversity," unworthy of his nature. In New York in 1951, Dahlberg writes his friend Sir Herbert Read that he does not approve of his way of living. "Do you think it is good to go to the foes of art to heal the artist? I don't care what money you get for whom, what you are doing is at the bottom a sin." He warns Read that he lives too shrewdly, and that this is "the worst error of a poet." For man must thirst, and must remain in the company of those who are athirst, he writes; and even if solitude is "a great pain in the heart," still "a man must remain in the wilderness."

To read Dahlberg's two collections (*Epitaph of Our Time* and *The Edward Dahlberg Reader*) is to enter that wilderness and to be all but overwhelmed by his passionate chronicling of the un-remitting affront to the spirit which makes alienation the greatest peril to contemporary, sensitive man. The loneliness and the separateness which result from this affront are apt to engender a climate favorable to art. Kafka wrote of the consequences of dis-esteem obliquely, his language German, his vehicle allegory, and startled the lost to a deeper recognition of how forsaken they were. Dahlberg, whose work may be compared to Kafka's in its intensity of discernment and foreboding, writes of that merciless assault on the spirit in cadenced, occasionally archaic, and consistently splendid English. His language is classic, his metaphor frequently myth, but both language and myth belong to him alone.

Kafka was, in his time, not only Germany's most disturbing but most reliable prophet. As an artist, he foretold with the mad-dest courage all the horror that was to come. Dahlberg, whose more than a dozen remarkable books have established a unique reputation for him in Europe as well as in America, deserves our recognition not only as a stylist, as critic, as poet but also as eloquent and unflinching prophet. He declares against the outrage to every sensibility that faces us at this moment whichever way we turn upon our native soil, and he grieves for the disaster that lies, still undefined, beyond the perilous rim of contemporary American violence. What modern man calls progress, Dahlberg recognizes (with Yeats) as the dying of men's hearts. He sees the degradation of love and learning everywhere.

The ambiguous self in relation to history, to country, to sex, and to eternity is furiously alive in all Dahlberg's work, but it is in his letters that that self emerges in all its restless continuity. The letters are pages torn from the annals of his nights and days, his hopes and griefs, and transmuted into the actual substance of com-passion, understanding, and yearning for those who are for the moment beyond the reach of his hand. "Bill Williams, you know, had another small stroke; I tremble for him, and also weep for him," Dahlberg writes to Josephine Herbst in 1958. "He has done so many things of which I disapprove, but how little I want to go on rebuking him. Poor, poor Bill, he is much too close to Nature. I would kill Nature could I save him."

But despite the sincere passion of his declared love, there is all too often a wariness in his approach to those whom he addresses, a lurking overzealousness that leaves one with the feeling that every human relationship Dahlberg has had was, without exception, a heartbreak to him in the end. At the very moment that he declares himself, he appears to tremble at the prospect of another devastating experience, still another emotional catastrophe from which he will never quite recover. "What the two of you cannot know," he writes to Allen Tate in 1965, "is that I fear going to other people's homes, and when I do, I leave as fast as I can, without seeming rude. It is not that I do not care deeply for my friends, or that I prefer to be with flimsy acquaintances rather than with the aristocratic intellects of our world. I dread unknowable disaster."

Lawrence Durrell once wrote a number of letters to Henry Miller on the subject of the artist's fear of accepting his own identity. He cited to Miller "Cézanne's fear that society would get the grappins on him . . . Gaugin's insistence on what the hell of a fine billiards player he was . . . and D. H. Lawrence fervently knitting, knitting, and trying to forget *Sons and Lovers*"—and there was Miller himself eating like mad to establish a reputation for himself as a gourmet. "Here are numberless types," Durrell wrote, "of the same ambiguous desire on the part of the artist to renounce his destiny. To spit on it." This was not for the moment Dahlberg's desire or dilemma. He knew from the beginning who he was and that he was destined, both as man and writer, to be an exile in the land of his birth. "First in the wanton streets of Kansas City," he writes to William Carlos Williams in 1957, "then in an orphanage, and then a waif of letters in New York." His dilemma, rather, was *how* to be a writer, and he studied the works of others avidly, seeking to find that way.

From the time of the appearance of his first novel, *Bottom Dogs,* published in 1929, there could be no question but that he had found his own exceptional speech. The Job of American letters, one critic has called him; and others have termed his autobiography, *Because I Was Flesh,* a masterpiece and "one of the few important American books published in our day." "The truth is," this outsized figure of American literature writes almost in panic to his friend Allen Tate (from Mallorca in 1962), "that I am a great coward before I dare venture one sentence. No man goes to the guillotine with greater apprehension than I sit down at my desk, no longer with a quill or a pen, but with a fell machine. . . . " For to Dahlberg a book is "a battle of the soul and not a war of words."

Leon Edel recently took Joyce to task for calling out in his letters for help, love, and money. Dahlberg's letters appeal for these same solaces. Is the artist to be reproached for articulating the constant cry of all living men? Is he not rather to be cherished for having spoken it so eloquently? And is not the attempt to answer that despairing cry the reason for all teaching, all learning, all writing, from the Greeks to Abelard, from the Old Testament to Joyce?

The voices of Camus and Sartre, Faulkner and Hemingway no longer reach the young in the far journey they are taking; and Salinger, who was once their spokesman, is now more silent than the tomb. This wayfaring generation, hair long on the shoulders and wounded faces staunched by beards, murmurs of Allen Ginsberg, Timothy Leary, and Bob Dylan, uncertain as to whether these saviors (or even William Burroughs and John Rechy) are saying fearlessly and honestly enough the words that must somehow be said. Born in 1900, Dahlberg offers a philosophy of rebellion, but of dignity and discipline as well, to the young who have the insight to look his way. That philosophy, strong and undismayed, is stated in almost every page he writes. It is there in "The Tragedy of American Love" and in "Heart Speaketh to Heart," both of which are included in *The Edward Dahlberg Reader*. It is there in his uncompromising letters, and strikingly there in his essay, "Thoreau vs. Contemporary America," in which he extends his hand to the uneasy, saying:

We are fatalists only when we cease telling the truth, but, so long as we communicate the truth, we move ourselves, life, history, men. There is no other way. This is the simple epitome of the wisdom of nonresistance to evil. It is what Confucius, Thoreau, and Tolstoi taught. It is the incredible, the visionary way, and it announces treason and betrayal more boldly than firearms or airplanes.

"IN APRIL, 1912, WHEN HE WAS ELEVEN, THE BOY BECAME INMATE 92 OF THE JEWISH ORPHAN ASYLUM IN CLEVELAND, THE FOREST CITY." *(BECAUSE I WAS FLESH,* CHAPTER 3)

ARNO KARLEN

Unfortunately, I know Edward Dahlberg. I could read him better before I met him. His work, like each artist's, presents a persona —his living self magnified through a distorting lens. This feature grows, that one vanishes, others sharpen, roughen, soften. Person and persona are as different as bootprint in the snow and naked foot. Were Dahlberg just a friend, I'd write about the person. But if a garland is gathered, it's because of his persona's greatness. So I write of that.

The persona, by its nature, is a paradox. It's the man, it's not the man—as one can equally say "Paris is France" or "Paris isn't France." Good introduction to Dahlberg's persona, for it's more riddling than most. Dahlberg (the persona) is the great, gorgeous crank of his age. All cranks are reactionaries, yet Dahlberg is a true modern, as unique in voice and form as any wild rebel of his generation. He lectures, he rants, he rhapsodizes—in a tongue part old, part modern, part invented—on a free-form dais done in rich old faded fustian. In long-dead cadences and eclectic diction, he makes baroque meanders from irony to oracle to lyric. He writes classic aphorisms and sprawling prose poems, moves the library into the street, the street into the past. At once one wonders. Is he like Pound, writing from and for his age in ancient speech? Or the opposite, like Spenser, man of an age past, talking oldly in his own day's tongue?

Impossible to say. One can't read his references to Eusebius and Bernal Diaz without spotting a cultural bank, with all the banker's conserving spirit—money, culture, it makes no difference. Then one sees the unarchitected rambles, the jangling rhetorics and symbols of ten ages, even his own; and one knows him for one of those headlong modern pillagers of all that makes for stunning dissonance, collage. So, again, is he like Dreiser rehashing Balzac or like Joyce ravishing Homer? No saying: he remains paradox.

Paradox again because this lonely, singular voice in American letters is crankish, and crankishness is at once a prison and a dare —its success more paradoxic still. Small crankishness is ridiculous, but great, spirited cranks make grand personae. Every crank is ruled by an obsession, which confines him; but his very bow to narrow bounds is an audacity. The greater the depth and richness of the obsession, the more narrow its conservatism—and therefore the more slashing the radicalism, the more breathtaking the tight-wire dance to greatness. A man with the courage of his obsession —that is, its total victim—plunges into risks of absurdity and grandeur that the balanced don't allow, and rightly.

Dahlberg's obsession is to create a mythological net to catch him in his fall toward death. An American, an artist, a Jew, a fatherless boy (I still mean the persona), he bounces as he walks the earth, without the ballast of inherited myth, longing for even the memory of a homeland and ancestral house. But even the memory is forgotten, teasing on the tip of his mind, so it cries for recreation every day in his work. The recreation is part guess, part invention, part the memory of remembering. So it is never right. The best success fails and makes him try again. So he remains an artist. And in his art he proves that an American, an artist, a Jew, a fatherless son lives out the myth of mythlessness, itself a Sargasso homeland.

So Dahlberg ransacks others' spirits, minds, remains, and homelands for a harmony, a *déjà vu*, a goading flash of recognition. He finds them in the Hill of Hebron, Kansas City's cattle grandees and succulent lady barbers, in Eusebius, Diaz, and Dreiser, in the stones of Mallorca and his mother's bones. The courage, pathos, and loveliness of his work all grow from this: he has created a mythology without a people. It has only a person. Edward Dahlberg.

WILLIAM O'ROURKE

> *Kansas City is a vast inland city, and*
> *its marvelous river, the Missouri,*
> *heats the senses.*
> —Because I Was Flesh

> *But he said unto them, All men*
> *cannot receive this saying, save they*
> *to whom it is given.*
> —Matt. 19:11

Kansas City was never vast to me and, not knowing either shelf of the continent, *inland* had no meaning. The river Missouri was reported as a suicide ditch; the newspaper carried inky photos of police with malignant grappling hooks. The city and I share the heavy wastrel days of my youth—the memories of childhood which are the phantom pains of the amputee. The Church was a gray proctor, but it gave me gold, frankincense, and myrrh. Kansas City is a market town with belligerent exhausts of monster trucks, battered ramps of loading docks, and the weak-colored, thrice-copy bill of lading. Most men's histories are written in bill receipts. Kansas City feels the waves of the Nation around it, the tossed stone that does not cause the ripples but is impressed by them.

"Homer sang of many sacred towns in Hellas which were no better than Kansas City." Edward Dahlberg returned to the city of

74

his youth to teach at the University of Missouri at Kansas City the spring of 1965; his audience were creative paupers, for I was one of them.

Women filled his classes. Cameoed dowagers with rouged jowls and red velvet capes, young brittle-lipped girls whose pens took notes nodding like steadfast crochet needles. A fluorescent insect hum came from the lighting fixtures in the large room, terraced with rows of chairs with wide spatula arms. The University had the charm of the nondescript. Originally a small private institution, it had a few simple sandstone buildings with red clay gable roofs—"pigeons had a universe in their eaves." I moved about the buildings with the vacant motions of a vagrant. My education has a Jesuitical residue and at eighteen the difference between the Spanish Civil War and the Franco-American War (which I adopted from a can of spaghetti) was not yet clear.

The draft in the corridors raised the fabric around the wrist that February. Edward Dahlberg came into the room in a heavy umber coat, mounted a creaking pine dais, was introduced by the head of the English Department, who listed his books soon to be published. Patches of white hair lay across his head; above a frieze of mustache was the strong nose, as galling as the golden calf. He announced that this would be no class of dry syntax; rather he would have us read truthful books which would quicken our pulses and dilate our sensibilities. These were not the regions where books were taken by the nervous nonce lives of his students. Taught as young critics they demanded the incest of fiction. There is no misfortune esteemed as a novel—an image to a primitive people has more power than the life it represents. A man of strong parts will be shunned, whereas the thinnest fictions will pulse, transfused with the plasma of Professors. Homer said the last song is always applauded the loudest; the students were in the din of the continual midst. The ancients and sages are considered the brackish past for the word *quote,* and its usage has become inhuman. It now denotes a bloodless severance. Phrases are put in quotation marks to disavow them in scorn or to allow the impasse to realize itself in print. We are provided with adages, truisms, and the gnomic line, but like the doubtful chiropractors they manage to crack our backs but do not give us spines. Edward Dahlberg partakes of the multiple rhythm of the blood of the writers who were as anonymous to his students as he was.

Edward Dahlberg told his class if they would read the *Compleat Angler* they would be more quiet. The masters' candidates were concerned with dredging up Faulkner, whom Dahlberg refused to discuss as "the literary figure of the Century," as one graduate student was wont to put it, because it was an ordeal to read his books. A lathy Navy veteran asked him a bogus question about Oriental Art, its suggestive qualities and its relationship to our abstract painting. He paused to let the hiss of sophistry out between the words of his question, which contained the antithetical approach he considered Edward Dahlberg's prose to have. The class waited, alerted.

He answered that he did not know enough about Oriental Art to instruct the fellow, except that as Lao-tze uses a slight linen manner and is in no way an elliptical mind so he believed their art to be. The filling-in the student allowed himself was the blending of his own empty spaces. He then told of an afternoon he spent with the painter Willem de Kooning in De Kooning's Third Street apartment. The painter stood at a window that looked down upon an alley of corrugated ashcans, wet, unhealthy skin of cardboard, sunken cellar windows agape like severed lower jaws and exclaimed to the persons in the room:

"Isn't it beautiful?" with a smeary sincerity.

Dahlberg showed simple horror at this and told De Kooning, "Children could not help but be maimed if they have such sights scratching across their memories," and quit his company.

Papers were read on novels we had selected which, as he advised us, were not sufficiently bad to be a book publisher's preface. The numbers in the room started to lessen; none returned with a green bough. Two wantons with yellow teeth and pants with brass zippers for their gentle central seam missed his classes because even they fell under a reproachment. The older women whose memories loosened as their vessels collapsed fell off from the front row where they commanded his gaze if not his imagination. But as I would pass out of the building I often saw him walking with a straight-limb girl who had always spoken in a soft manner. I never said a word to her, though during the recitations of student papers her bowed back eased my *rigor mortis* contemplations.

He recommended all of Sherwood Anderson, so a few papers were written on *Winesburg, Ohio* and *Poor White.* The night before, he told us, he visited a home where the child of the family kissed his hand. He was very moved, for he told it twice. A paper was then read by a boy on *Poor White,* which was dim sociology. Dahlberg asked why he did not include the meaning of the seed, the machinery invented to harvest it, and the sterile seed he delivered to his wife. The boy had not pondered this and was not concerned with how much love or "hot sperm" went into the making of a child. When Anderson's own lines were read Edward Dahlberg would lean back, close his eyes, and say:

"Yes, very good. Thank you."

Edward Dahlberg would nod his head while his thumbs muttered at his waist and thank the young person who would repeat such lines to let him dwell on and release their powers to his listeners.

In his creative writing class there were some two dozen students. Women in the special education division who took these courses so their wells of sensibility might be dipped into. One businessman was included who sat immobile in a corner chair with a suit the color of corrosion. His face had a translucent skin which showed catacombs of veins, red and periwinkle. He was auditing and seemed comfortable in this position. Throughout the semester he offered only the diction of pleasantries and finally Edward Dahlberg asked him if he might do a paper. The men spoke and his awry face flamed:

"I've worked for my company twenty years and I have had eighteen electric shock treatments. . . ."

He stopped and began grasping air with his mouth. Dahlberg sat at his desk in a plain of silence that followed whereon passed annals of intrusions of suffering. He said:

"I am very sorry for you."

The man never reappeared.

Edward Dahlberg only forsook a lecture when he was in need of a physician. The head of the English Department announced this and called for remarks about the author in residence. After their objections he told the students Dahlberg was fond of using inkhorn words, which was an enema synthesis they found a comfort.

The writing class had decomposed to a half dozen. Another male, a speech teacher of twenty-four who needed the credit to get his master's degree in order to teach some hapless students the next year, and an assortment of female poets. Dahlberg sat with his legs crossed with gray exhaustion over his face and the tops of his unraveling many-colored socks exposed when a woman volunteered to read a children's book she had written. He had spoken against the children's dilutions of the Classics before, but consented with alarm for there was no other offering during the period. She began:

"Winnie was a puppy who looked like a mop and rode the elevators of downtown Kansas City until everybody knew his name. . . ."

Edward Dahlberg, American artist, sat with his head shrouded by his hands.

She continued:

"He would walk around the Plaza, for he lived with his master in an apartment. . . ."

"Stop," he said, hardly audible. "Stop. Please."

The panes in the building's long windows were mottled and May filled these thin pools with color. Only after asking permission would Edward Dahlberg read from his own works and this late in the semester. He read from *The Sorrows of Priapus:*

Socrates described love as the sting of a tarantula. We see that desire dominates the old as well as youth; the senile forget to button their clothes, and leave the door of their trousers ajar. . . .

He stopped and looked up at his class of housewives and the one young man, who "desperately wanted to have feelings."

78

"Why do you stop?" asked one of the mothers from the back of the room.

He hesitated, but turned the pages from the spot and replied:

"You should be frank on paper, but I'll decline to read this passage aloud."

He had once before remarked on the Scottsboro case—the verdict of which I knew nothing about—saying, if he could be pardoned:

"I would not use the washroom after the woman involved."

Justice was within that remark and, I thought, in the measure of his balance that knew a frank page and could find reason to leave it be.

In the larger class the Navy veteran asked again a question with an impertinent unction on it, but quoted a line from the autobiography in doing so. After hearing his words come from the man's lips Edward Dahlberg said:

"Since you remember what I have written, I have seeped into your soul and it will take you quite a few years to realize what that means."

The veteran was silenced as were the others as he remained thrust out over his desk, the pine bending aloud while under his weight.

He often said, "Read my books, don't look to me." When someone would say an agreeable thing about him he said, quoting Prince Myshkin, "Thank you very much for liking me." In the writing class delivered by a *deus ex machina* adviser there was the "Miss Missouri" of that year. She was the daughter of a talented family who would tour counties playing at fairs, livestock shows, and, in larger cities, nightclubs. Their traveling bus had large gleeful letters of advertisement on its side. She played more than one instrument and more than one at a time. She wrote a paper on *Madame Bovary* and defended Emma, which Dahlberg amended and reminded her it was Flaubert who said, "I am Madame Bovary." She had a peculiar way of standing which amounted to a contestant's at attention. Her smile was as ready as an opening curtain. She was absent frequently because of the family's raucous touring and Dahlberg had been asking her to perform for the class if she refused to write more papers. He finally shamed her into doing a song, which she did in a timely up-tempo fashion, tapping her thigh, standing forthrightly but without the aid of her silk "Miss Missouri" bandolier. She sat down after applause and the meager looks of the other women and asked Edward Dahlberg if he would sing—the same number, for it was an old one. He tipped back his chair, raised his jaw, and, making a rapids of his throat, sang. And he sang!—a slow original blues version of the tune. He often grieved he could no longer see the image of his mother before him. I grieve that I can't remember the simple verses of the song he sang before us.

When I last shook his hand I was sure of quitting school. I had his book, unread, *Alms for Oblivion,* which I asked him to inscribe. He did, bending low above the page, for his "sight is starved." I looked into his face then; the left eye had turned a robin's-egg blue and the other, which caught into you as he said:

"I sympathize with your predicament, as you know I must, but you should stay in school lest you become entangled by Sears Roebuck."

All I knew was that he had seeped into my soul and I no longer could follow the shambles of his figure silently down the steps of that midland university.

He returned to Kansas City the following semester and became ill; having no quickened students he left shortly after. A small editorial in the student newspaper complained of the money the English Department paid him, about half the price of a Chevrolet. In a public lecture he gave to Kansas City he said that for those who did not read his books, "It was their loss."

He had given out a list of books that he wanted his students to read, not for the class but during their whole lives, for these were such books. His classes, too, were for his students' whole lives; but the stories of his friends Dreiser, Anderson, and Crane, his beloved Ford Madox Ford were only place-names to his listeners. "I sing of Oak, Walnut, Chestnut, Maple, and Elm Streets." Ford Madox Ford called it jocund fate, but is this what returned Edward Dahlberg to Kansas City, a town that "nursed men, mules, and horses as famous as the asses of Arcadia"?

Edward Dahlberg was bleached in a town that is still green and meadowed; I too neglected him there, though I now know that Kansas City has its living region in Edward Dahlberg. It is he who has a vast inland city and the marvelous river that heats the senses.

THE HOUSE ON MCGEE STREET
(SINCE LEVELED IN AN URBAN RENEWAL PROJECT)

WILLIAM M. RYAN: *The house on McGee*

When you take Edward Dahlberg riding in your metal cage the town he discovers through the smothered glass is not exactly to be found by anyone else. The newer mansions, the office hives,* even the baroque artifacts of former splendor he hardly sees at all. Or trees and plantings. What fills a scene for him is what the rest of us tend to ignore, or at most we think of some poor old house: "Real value $7,000.00; $75.00 a month." Not Edward. The moment he sees one that's been left to stand in a reconstructed block he says, "Isn't that a handsome old house?"

You almost ask him why he had passed the wooden palaces of Victorian gingerbread with scarcely a glance, for the houses that warm his eye are of two storeys, not three or four. Their sides are lean, and ornaments, if any, are spare. They were made of heavy bricks or seasoned pine, with woodwork inside of walnut or cherry or gumwood or even golden oak and floors of edge-grain oak. All of it material that a "higher class" of people today could never afford. Yet his type of building bears no sign of opulence.

When they were new, these small dwellings had more simple dignity and modesty than the men and women who built them.

* Of a new building on the campus of the University of Missouri at Kansas City: "It looks like a mausoleum. They should have buried the architect in it."

Today, ill-tenanted and rundown, they add some touch of grace to drabness. A tiny percentage of these straight-backed houses are invisibly glorified by having been lived in by someone who became famous. In this regard the ancient brick at Eighth and McGee is one of them, for here lived Edward Dahlberg and his mother Lizzie from 1901 to 1906. Structurally it does not fit the Dahlberg canon, being a small apartment building with a stone facade. But it is neat and simple in outline, and the sight of it recalls angled homes under arching shade.

It might be surmised that the sexagenarian would retrace his boyish paths, up the front steps with their stout rock walls, around the yard, through the narrow hallways inside, to the room where his mother (forever beloved) cooked for him. But no such thing.

One day in 1965 Edward asked me to drive him downtown and see if we could find the old house. It was still there, standing alone and locked in the ice field of concrete and parking-lot asphalt. The planes were straight as ever—rows of stone and bricks and mortar, pinched lintels, unlofty ridges at the top. The only irregularity was a homely washing in the dooryard.

Edward called our attention to its architectural soundness and levelness after more than a century of hard use. (It remained, even after a bad fire in 1966.) He said he hoped it would be spared the wrecker's ball.

Judging by the clothes on the line someone was probably at home. Would he like to go in?

He answered carelessly, "I don't think so."

No mooning over notches in woodwork and windowsills where a dreaming boy had once leaned out. No sir. Of sentiment for something once possessed Dahlberg has as little as a Trappist. The house was of passing interest to him chiefly because the sight of it brought clear memories of decorums and styles that are gone except for a few pathetic shells. The world was a thousand years younger then. Pride held up an honest head among carpenters and masons, and there was kinship between their hands and the wood and clay of the earth.

84

ADELE Z. SILVER: *Excerpts from "Father of Beatnik Novel 'Discovered' "*

He used the years of withdrawal, which he describes in terms of near-religious solitude, to turn himself into a writer and his writing into literature. They were years of reading, of finding a style to match the roiling feelings inside him.

In several conversations and letters, Dahlberg and I talked about that time, his ideas, style, and second success. What did he read then, I asked, and what does he read now?

"The same, the masters of wisdom. In a morning I go to the epigrams of Horace, the poems of Catullus, the *Moralia* of Plutarch; and on another, to Philo Judaeus, or the Babylonian Talmud, or to Hakluyt's *Voyages* and Buffon. All this I tell you at the risk of sounding pretentious, but you have asked me what I read and I am giving you a plain answer."

How do you feel, I asked cautiously, about your life as a writer? His laugh was thin. "So few understand the predicament of the writer in our land today. You sit at your guillotine desk, you wonder if somewhere you have readers. I am not discontented with my portion, since I never wrote a line for lucre. But even the pensive maggot expects his supper."

Oh, but surely, I protested, these last few years must mean you'll have a little money and comfort? The laugh was heartier. "One of my publishers, James Laughlin at *New Directions,* a fantastically rich man, has been very courageous and has brought out many valorous volumes others might never have considered.

"But he expects authors to eat fame, a very indigestible supper. He once said to me, 'Edward, money is my Cross,' and I replied, 'James, couldn't I carry it a while for you?' The publishers of

Horizon Press, Ben Raeburn and Coburn Britton, who is from Cleveland, do not fail to see that even a truthful writer must eat, have a roof, and be able to buy books."

In *Bottom Dogs* and again in *Because I Was Flesh,* Dahlberg told of his years, 1912–17, in the Jewish Orphan Asylum in Cleveland. His account still annoys many supporters of the old asylum, now Bellefaire, and Dahlberg is still surprised.

"I am sorry that the people at the former JOA so totally misconceived my feeling toward my experience there. . . . I was not glutted with hate, as some surmise, but had only one motive, and that was to tell the truth as artistically as I could. . . . That I have never expunged those tender and humiliating years there is apparent."

Dahlberg has other vivid memories of Cleveland: "One of the most piercing moments at Central High School came unexpectedly one day, when I had the regal occasion to talk to my teacher in a class of English. All that I remember is that she had a marvelous cairn of red hair (and according to William Morris a commonwealth of such women was sufficient cause to believe in a utopia), and she said to me, 'You are going to be somebody on this earth.'

"It was the only praise I had ever received during that lacerated boyhood in an asylum twenty thousand leagues distant from Elysium.

"I regarded Euclid Avenue as the Field of Asphodels, but what that street is now I do not know. But then I imagined that city a marvelous windy Trojan town. I remember it a city of trees and it still is a vine in my blood."

I thought it kindest to remain silent.

He now lives in a New York apartment—"we took it because it has ample space for books"—on a Lower East Side street, whose name jogged my memory of his autobiography. Didn't your mother once live there, I asked, on the same street? Now it was his turn to be silent for a moment. "You're right," he replied. "I had forgotten. Our beginnings and our ends are the same after all."

↓ EDWARD

Greetings from Class of 1917

Mrs. Ben Kasner
Jennie Berg
Edna Bergman
Mrs. Arthur Bergman
Mrs. Ida Lewis
Minnie Davidson
Ruth Feldman
Rose Goldstein
Mrs. N. Kutler
Sarah Levy
Mrs. Anne Wolfson
Mrs. Rose Price
Lucille Marcus
Zelda Morris
Mrs. Wm. Roth
Sally Scheingold
Rose Schwartz
Mrs. Jack Liebowitz
Grace Theiner
William Roth
Max Rotter
Dave Rosenthal

Sam Anderman
Fred Bartell
Wm. Bloomberg
Sam Corenman
Edward Dalberg ✔
Arthur Ellman
Louis Fellhandler
William Feldman
Eli Friedman
Joe Gabriel
Max Glassman
Harry Goldstein
Max Harris
Max Herman
Jack Klapper
Jack Lewis
Ben Malross
Sol Perelman
Edward Prager
Abe Segal
Albert Silverglade
Ben Weisman

"WE CAN DIGEST OUR CHILDHOOD BUT NEVER OUR PRESENT DEEDS,
BECAUSE NO ONE KNOWS WHAT HE IS DOING WHILE HE IS DOING IT. . . .
THE DAY OF LEAVING THE HOME HAD COME. HE STOOD ON THE STAGE
IN THE PRAYER HALL AND SANG THE DIRGE OF SEPARATION TOGETHER
WITH THE OTHER ORPHANS WHO WERE IN THE CONFIRMATION CLASS
OF 1917." (BECAUSE I WAS FLESH, CHAPTER 3)

DONALD J. PAQUETT.

A good name is better than precious ointment.—Ecclesiastes

He came to my old house on the hill many memories ago, bearing greetings from a young poet back East; he was neatly but cheaply dressed—hatless, coatless, smiling—and he was hungry. Mother prepared a good lunch, a long talk followed—about poetry mostly —then we went for a ride. Having learned that I had never finished grammar school and having scanned the gaudy volumes on my shelves with a series of grunts and frowns, he suggested that we stop at the nearest bookstore. Three afternoons there—after we searched the shelves of dealers near and far—finding, at last, Anderson, Aeschylus, Burton, Bruyère, Blake, Donne, Ovid, Gilbert White, Isaac Walton, old Sam Johnson, and armfuls of others, many of whom I had never heard of. Later in his small upstairs apartment in Santa Monica we talked many times of the giants of literature, but never of the dwarfs. Verily I would rather face a famished tiger in a field of thorns and briars than mention the name of some celebrated lord-of-language or "dollar-scribbler" in his presence. Hearing a trite word or phrase would often bounce him into the hard lap of instant wrath, and the mere mention of a bad book would plunge his brooding soul into infernal depths.

Cooking was another thing. When Edward leaned over the antique stove he was helpless as a plucked pullet. Lord, the fun I had watching him fuss and fumble as he fixed my dinner. Either

88

he would burn the toast or the egg; often he would blacken both. The coffee would bubble out the crooked spout, and he would forget all about the usual avocado he had planned to serve. Poor, dear Edward—I never knew anyone to whom literature meant so much. I didn't always agree with him, and on a few memorable occasions I stood up and told him so. It was like challenging the wrath and wisdom of God Almighty himself. I have seen him hard and bitter as a burnt almond, heard him hailed *windbag, moaning Caesar,* and *lord scavenger of antiquity.* Once or twice, in my folly, I agreed. But I took a second look—a third! Later, when he left the country, I returned and stood outside the old weeping house, wondering where and how he was, wishing he were back again.

Years later he returned and spent a few days with my wife and me here at the old house on the hill. Again I was glad to see him; again he squinted frownfully over my books and bemoaned the absence of some of his old immortals still missing from my shelves. Again and yet again he grimly admonished me, "Read good books, work hard; it is the only way. Donald, you are still a fool, but I have not given up hope for your future."

Later, at his rented summer cottage in Santa Barbara, we renewed our friendship, and the following year my wife and I came again. Once we arrived early—while the old walrus was still hard at work. But never again, for we found him full of frosts and frowns. It was like trying to get along with a sea lion at mating season. O he was mean to me at times, or so I thought; and, frankly, I know of no kindred soul whose friendship he has not bruised or blemished at one time or another. But enough now of that.

The silt has sluiced down the trough of time—the glory and the gold remain. Like an enduring oak hidden in a dark forest this son of Moses and the immortal barber from the bottomlands of Missouri has grown during the years. It has been many months since I saw him last. Still I miss him. Now and then he sends a small letter of comfort and consolation, urging me on and on, not to yield to darkness and despair. "Read good books, work hard; it is the only way."

GILBERT SORRENTINO

The first of Edward Dahlberg's books to come to my attention was the Harcourt, Brace edition of *Do These Bones Live*. I still remember the excitement and awe with which I read this beautiful and pure work, so remote from what I had come to think was "criticism," yet critical in the very best sense of that word. That book (and subsequently the rest of Dahlberg's work) seemed such a clear-sighted attack on the chicanery and guile of American life as to literally be its own explanation; i.e., there was nothing to which the work could be compared. I would say, unhesitatingly, that Edward Dahlberg has been a great influence on me, not, certainly, in any sense of "style" or "philosophy" but in a broader sense of placing the anguish of the America of the twentieth century clearly in the light.

Some time later I met Edward Dahlberg, during his sojourn in New York, and talked with him many times. I clearly recall one evening, when Edward was visiting at my house along with a number of my friends—all members of my own generation—and I remember how he "tolerated" us, the only word I can think of to describe his generous stance. Oh, we knew it all in those days! And Edward was a strange throwback to a time when a writer showed

90

respect and deference to his elders: curious aberration. We thought that we had nothing to learn from him and that his presence among us was an indication that he hoped to learn from us—who had nothing at all to teach. Now, with humiliation, I see that this very great man had come to us out of loneliness and out of some need to sustain himself as an artist in the company of fellow artists—neophytes though we were—thirty years his junior.

How kind he was. And with what elegance he graced our table. Another poet and I asked him if he knew an ancient song, "Hello Central, Give Me No-Man's-Land," a popular tune of the First World War. Without a moment's hesitation, Edward sang the song, in a gentle vaudeville manner. It was such an absolute gesture of candor, and love. We laughed to hide our shame at having thought to bait him.

To close this brief and inadequate note, let me say that he trusted and encouraged young writers, he listened to them, and his deviations from what was at that time our literary enthusiasm were salutary. To be absolutely clear about it, let me accord him what to me is the highest honor one can give a writer, or any artist, outside useful praise for work well done: Mr. Dahlberg, as Pound says of the temple, is holy, because he is not for sale.

DRAWING BY DAVID LEVINE. COPYRIGHT 1968,
NEW YORK REVIEW OF BOOKS.

RONALD JOHNSON: *"Be Primordial or Decay":*
Correspondence

These are selections from letters written by Edward Dahlberg to Jonathan Williams over a period of twelve years, 1955–67. I have kept their order intact, but within three sections: the first pertaining to relations between an older and a younger writer; the second concerned with the deserts and wildernesses of modern life; and the third, the dilemma of publishing. This is a somewhat unorthodox procedure, but on the whole the letters themselves fall naturally into these categories. There are of course exclusions, but I have tried everywhere to extract without changing the essential tone of this relationship.

Edward Dahlberg springs out of that thistle patch where once Thoreau tended his beans, and now there is the litter of motor courts and paved roads. Thoreau longed for a book "which shall push out with the skunk-cabbage in the spring," and Dahlberg has written it, its odor unmistakably moral, inescapable, primordial. The Emersons of our day fidget in the parlors, and talk of the properties.

There are both correspondences and differences between the two, but the "signature" is on the leaves of the plant: they believe, in Dahlberg's words, that it is impossible "to create a civilization in a land that covers more territory than the body of a Titan"; they are the self-appointed pariahs to this civilization, the gadflies of what is more titanic than Titan; and the prose they have developed is individual, prickly, as solitary as the mullein and as indigenous as sassafras. Thoreau withdrew to the woods, however. While Dahlberg, more cosmopolitan, more modern, engages himself, jousts at the windmills of his own humanity and the manners, erudition, politics, sex life, honesty, gullibility, and warmth of others. All in a style as close-packed, as variegated as the legendary ancestor of Indian corn. And as elusive. He declares in these letters: "It may take you a while to find your symbols, the air in Quito is sometimes too refined to breathe, but the heavens are lucid, and twilight there lasts no more than three seconds." It is, this extraordinary style, as rarefied as the air in Quito—or as pungent as the exhalations of the skunk cabbage. But we come to it, come back to it, in all its astringencies, as a tonic to our lives: the friends who no longer write letters, bemused by the apparent ease and distractions of newer communications; our daily investigations into the supermarket where there is no honest food to be bought; as a writer, our hopes for even a polite response from friends to whom we have sent our last book; the commercialism; the pandering; the newest delusions; and the hopelessness of the newest war fought for economic or personally strategic gains; the despair and necessity of America.

I wonder sometimes whether we deserve an Edward Dahlberg to reprimand us and cajole us. But he is not to be put off. His very genius is that he permeates us, apprehends us in our dreams and errors, like the perennial awakenings of some bitter and primordial spring. Thaw and crack, reader, or remain in your glacial decay.

R. J.

I. "HOW MUCH LOAM, ORDINARY DIRT, FOLIAGE, MOSS, AND EVEN DEAD CARCASSES OF BIRDS THAT ONCE WERE JUBILANT IS IN A BOOK"

February 7th, 1955

My own work on American and English Literature is almost done; I have nothing but abhorrence for the gigantic gnats of our Parnassus, and my own essays are largely denunciatory. There is not enough probity among the lot of these thieves to pass through the eye of a needle. In the times of Horace the prize for skill in verses was a goat, but how many obscure and plain writers ever earn as much.

January 18th, 1956

Your interest in Indian origins is very sound. We must gather up our own myths and translate them into parables and a fabled landscape for our lives and spirit. This is our Kabalah, and if men, like yourself, can abandon the affectations of Pound, the doggerel of Eliot, the fatuous banter of cummings, and write it in real English, archaic if necessary, but not low or cheap (we imagine that because we are colloquial we are local, historical, or even show any character), there is hope for American Literature. . . .

It may take you a while to find your symbols, the air in Quito is sometimes too refined to breathe, but the heavens are lucid, and twilight there lasts no more than three seconds. . . .

I have much confidence in you if you will continue to seek that mineral of El Dorado in our beginnings. Here is Alpha and Omega, the Gnostic One and Seven and our fate, which is the quest.

December 30th, 1957

As I belong to no literary merchants' sodality I do not know what will happen to my own book or where it will be reviewed. I have fought too many pecuniary street-gamins of literature to get balm or even the smallest moiety of justice from most places. Should you know where my book can be ventilated I should be grateful to you. Be sure, too, I have no venal motive. I simply want to be read by those readers so hidden from writers because of the cabals of imbecilic book reviewers of our daily locusts, the newspapers.

May 12th, 1958

I am at work on a narrative and I have not done a novel since 1934, and am also doing epistolary essays on Lawrence, James, Joyce, quite heterodoxical on my part, with Herbert Read. The *Nation* had taken three of my letters and three of Read's, had advertised them, and after keeping them for a year, was too pusillanimous to publish them.

94

It is absolutely fatuous to argue with the pallbearers of American casket periodicals. I have no time to waste on them. If you saw the piece of illiteracy misnamed a letter which I received from the *Nation* you would wince. All the rubbish that comes from trade, cupidity, and advertising is now known as the American Language. God spare us all. It's enough to have been born in the states without adding to that another cairn of griefs.

June 13th, 1958

How you managed to get a Guggenheim Award I don't know. They must have made a mistake. They have given their money to such louts, literary mercenaries, mastiffs on dunghills, that when it is offered to a person of genuine quality I need smelling salts.

August 3rd, 1958

The Irving Layton poems came today; I would care for this man had he more respect for his own talent. He is often foolish rather than witty. You must pardon me, I find a great deal of the vernacular affectation, stylized nonsense of the academy. Pound does not know anything about the language, the speech of the guttersnipe, and when he drops into jargon I need an emetic. I was brought up in the streets of a midwestern city, and you may or may not have read *Bottom Dogs,* and it does not matter, but at least you will see that I know what I am talking about. You cannot go far back into those ancestral realms of your own identity with a speech that is, in the main, coarse. When words are derived from agrarian or deeply human origins they have great, pulsing value. But look, now all these criminal urchins have discovered another neologism—for divorce, they say splitville, for tedium, dullville. This is a national madness, and what we must do is to revivify the language and not bring about its rot. . . .

Do not think that I set aside Layton's talent. There are lines that I like a good deal. He is afraid of being serious; one can be earnest without becoming a bore. One ought to be licentious in a more poetic vocabulary, as Catullus was or as was Petronius or the Chinese writers. What is the point of titling a book *XYZ* (which sounds like the stygian address in New York City, Avenue A) or *The Long Pea-Shooter?* It is not amusing, and will only put people off who otherwise would be his adherents. Still, it is good to know that someone in that frontier pitiless land, Canada, has feeling, and I hope he will explore his powers. We need poets desperately, and I think it is immoral of him to dung upon his own gifts by hiding his real sorrow, and even his tremendous lusts.

August 30th, 1958

I still think sooner or later you will have to get out of the vernacular though I do not doubt that some of the hill, mountain, and valley words which doubtless derive from Elizabethan English are very good. But one can be as pedantic about the patois as anything else or as foolish as Pound is. I committed three mistakes in the vernacular, that is, three novels. . . .

The only Masters I know are bastards. Once a woman living with Sherwood Anderson addressed him as "Master" whereupon he picked up his valise and left.

September 23rd, 1958

I believe you are a brave and talented man; give, if you don't think I am a pedagogue, enough time to season your own pulses with good, wise books. Try as best you can to link the past with today; otherwise you have all the raging buffoonery of Dada, which some may call surrealism, existentialism, or what the vulgarians now call the "beat generation." Everybody is defeated from the moment he quits his mother's womb. Soon as you are in the world, and granting that some centuries are worse than others, and we are at the bottom of the pit of Acheron, the struggle commences. What is important then is to find examples that will nourish other people and not kill them. Let Nature do that, and the task will be accomplished soon enough. . . .

I like you very much, and if you will heed me, since I have no screed to offer you, but a long humiliating experience, a thousand Golgothas, I may be of some use to you as a person and a writer. I am not looking for disciples. Jesus did not even know what to [do] with the apostles, and they had such dull auditory nerves that they could not hear what came from his soul. It is easier to walk on water as Peter did than it is to listen to another man. . . .

My situation is no different from yours. Maybe you think I am a successful writer. I can tell you that I loathe the word success. My dear good friend, Josephine Herbst, is inveighing against fame when she asserts that Bartram searched for the source of streams, gathered seeds, walked through unknown quagmires, scrutinized the leaves of the alder and the scrub-oak, not to be renowned, but because he had an overpowering love within himself which he wanted to give to others. Is a volume a seedling which may grow into an aspen, a plane tree or a birch within you? If nothing grows after you have read a book then you have had a baleful and dismembering experience. Do we have to go to books to be assassinated? How much loam, ordinary dirt, foliage, moss, and even the dead carcasses of birds that once were

96

jubilant is in a book. Whole islands that are composed of the dead are today the loam and ground of the living. Does a book awaken you? Will it bring you closer to another lorn person? You and I know the tragedy of separation, which we won't dissolve by palaver and beer at the Cedar Bar. It is a great purgative experience to be together provided that our purpose is mirthful or earnest or both and not just to be more sodden and inert.

February 1st, 1959
You ought to get back to the writing; that is the source of your melancholia. I am not setting aside the world and all the scurvy Iscariots in it, but those, like the whore and the poor, we will always have with us.

I have real belief in the book on Herbals; it takes a great deal of imagination to have come to such a wondrous ore and theme. And if it does not sound lofty or furtively patronizing I can only say that I never had the mind or the feeling to have thought of it myself when I was lucky enough to be your age.

We are all dupes, Jonathan, and only the shrewd who never feel anything, are never gulled; beware of a man who cannot be betrayed. Christ, the Word, was born to be deceived, and maybe this is not only our flesh, but to act contrary to it would be unnatural and base. . . .

I have no time to reread what I have done. I am too busy trying to write a good or a truthful line now. There are no laurels for what you have done in the past; in writing there is only now, as in life. Everything one has done is a sepulchre, and one is too afraid of looking at the corpse.

May 5th, 1959
Lucky a man does not recollect what he says. Simonides asserted that when he spoke he almost always regretted it, but when he did not he never did.

May 25th, 1959
I have been at the autobiography; for six weeks I was very stagnant, but reading, and now I am in a high gale of animal exuberance, and writing. Is it good. Who can tell, not I. . . . I cannot write any more quickly than my poor brain will allow. The words come only when the heart permits them to rise up out of the depths of one's chaos.

August 6th, 1960
I will also get a letter off to Paul Metcalf, a very charming nature, with wondrous understanding of those sources and fountainheads of America so little known and so precious to my spirit. Please ask him

to forgive me. You know I am not usually so uncivil. I would rather be dead than stuffed with the kind of success that would make me invulnerable to the acclivities and the oceans and the archipelagos of another human soul.

September 15th, 1960
One should come to the assistance of any one who has real talent, and who is not giving us the stale aesthetics on American jazz, baseball, John Dewey, television, radio and the newspaper. Keep, in other words, your own book on herbals free of this. You have a genuine lyrical gift, and if you want to be a fool, Jonathan, just as I have been, and can only be, be the sweet fool and the bitter fool of Lear, and not an American fool. . . .

You have, you know, as always, my genuine appreciation, and I am not afraid of that great tabu American word, gratitude. You are young, which does not mean that you are dull or stupid or idiotic, and I am much older, which does not signify that I am wise, humble or less of a cretin. What can we do? The best we can, with absolute mad Quixote vision; give me windmills in my brains, or take away my mind altogether.

November 16th, 1960
Do more on the Whitman poem. A remarkable approach. You are a very clever reader, Jonathan, beware! All of us have obscene souls but some words and sins must be kept as private as the grave, although I confess your diction is so good that lettered words fall out of your mouth like the honey of Hymettus.

December 15th, 1960
I have your piece on *Can These Bones Live,* and like it very much, very; the use of the Rilke line as the title for your essay pleases me also. You do well, Jonathan, to quote me against myself, done with eloquence and with justice. What a disorderly animal is man, and who am I to imagine that I am at best a peer, maybe, to the forlorn featherless biped.

March 11th, 1961
So, my dear Jonathan, you see that it does not matter how long we are in this wretched trade called writing, our difficulties are often the same, and if I have some advantages which you do not yet enjoy, well I have had to pay for it. You have to decay a great deal before you receive any recognition at all and if you want to be a truthful author you're in the Valley of Hinnom for all the days of your life. So now, at 60, I must look to you and to Paul [Carroll], and to others who

have wondrous sensibilities and gifts, to come to my rescue. I'll never be a safe man for anybody or any magazine.

July 8th, 1961
Please forgive me for not writing to you far earlier. I have had mountainous difficulties with the autobiography, and now, without any nonsensical bombast, Jonathan, I have to take a morning off to send a couple of letters to friends, you, and two others, which means I can't work this day. But please do not regard this as a bad remark, since I feel uneasy mentioning it. I am doing portraits of men in Paris, including Hart Crane, whom I knew, and for whose work and tragedy I have the utmost compassion. That will finish the first volume of *Because I Was Flesh,* and then I must write, burn the chaff of which there is doubtless much, and pray that I am not the greatest ass who ever wrote his memoirs. . . .

As for the introduction [to the reprint of *Bottom Dogs*] I did not want to do a long piece, nor did I wish to seem unsympathetic with the college of obscenity and ordure; it is I feel a great mistake, but I understand the reasons for it; it has always been the same; the Paris expatriates were doing the same thing. There is a great deal of blagueur about the '20's, the '30's and so on; it takes millions of years to produce a gnat, and if punctuation ⌐ ̄yntax alter a little in so miserable space of time as four lustra what difference does that make to our mortal dilemmas, to the anguish of just being disorderly, suffering flesh and not being able to do anything about it.

December 23rd, 1961
Along with *Bottom Dogs* came your brilliant piece in *Chelsea Review* on *Can These Bones Live;* I can tell without any canting nonsense, Jonathan, that in the past few years I can count on one hand the number of serious and contemplative essays on my work, and yours, along with Herbert Read's, Allen Tate's and Paul Carroll's, will be worth reading ten years hence. The other day a charming editor of one of the Dublin papers sent me a review of the book done by Herbert Read and myself; it was in the *Manchester Guardian,* and although the man who wrote it was clever and discerning, and the piece was altogether to my advantage, it could hardly be called literary criticism. You have to wait for another poet, like yourself, to value your books; otherwise, what is the guerdon for writing, except in the work itself; only you can't resurrect it as you can grass, wheat, or a river, just by looking at it; it withers after a short while, and you don't know whether the book has died or you are dead; in short, something has expired, and you don't have the scantiest need of a book written four lustra ago, or even

a year ago. Everything is chaff in my mouth; I am talking of my own writing, and without you, it would not have as much life for me as the quietly breathing ephesian sod.

January 14th, 1962
Every time we compose one good line a forest springs up in our hearts.

January 22nd, 1962
We both drain our hyssop to the lees; what else can we do? But there is good luck too, a very fickle angel. Remember there is no time though the Seraph in the Apocalypse had to swear that there would be none in Paradise, and so we have to wait and be patient; the guillotine comes anyway for Villon, you and me, and all others who are foolish enough to have feelings.

February 17th, 1962
As for the *Literary Review,* and as for who is important, is it not always a gnat, a man who has no talent, and no character, who is always prattling about importance. What is significant in this life? Suppose I write a remarkably honest book, imagine that it has genius, who will believe it, and after four persons admit it, you are in the gutter of limbo anyway, or if you are a successful brach of literature, why that is worse, you are less than a worm, you imagine that because 12 unimportant people said you were as gifted as Euripides you are most willing to confess this to everybody you meet, and upon the first occasion you have.

March 1st, 1962
The autobiography should be finished within a month. It took me well over 2 years to write it, and now another half a year to throw away the stubble, and hope afterwards there is some Gold of Ophir left.

Delacroix once said: "I write for myself alone," but I don't think we write for anybody, just as we die for nobody either. I write because I have nothing better to do and nothing worse. The predicament is the same for all of us, and I just haven't the time or the strength to spend my days trying to be famous. . . .

Anyway, we should bring some table-salt, and a sheaf of wild weeds and offer them to the god of failure. It's the only deity worth respecting nowadays. Soon as a man becomes too successful he is an untouchable. He doesn't want to be contaminated by broken-down poets and gifted obscurians. The world was made for the shrewd, and for that reason I have little regard for good manners, ror no one is so polite and dead as a venal scribbler. Well, all this you know, and as for the

Cedar Bar, that was never a very nourishing nightmare. I prefer bad dreams, and a great bundle of darkness, which I can use as a legend or my daily viaticum.

March 12th, 1962
You have such a clever ear for language that you must guard against it. Only the other day I was perusing a book by a rich nature, whom I cannot recall at the moment, who spoke of the limits of wit. God knows, we have so little of this metaphysical stuff nowadays in the universal Babel, that I ought to thank you very much for it. But there is another problem; of your genius I have no doubt . . . but are you using it deeply? Of course, in time you will please the so-called intelligentsia, and you very much please me. But I want more of the herbs; soon as you mention an ordinary vegetable you're a visionary. Of course, if anybody later wants to know how we spoke, and all the quick and undersided locutions of the day, then [they] can find that out from you, and you will be profoundly rewarding. Before I cite you, let me say there are many random lines and half lines that linger in my brain, but which you will some day more fully resolve. Shall I say, my friend, as you immature. A hideous word, maturity, and only a coward will use it. . . .

So take your wonderful wit, but don't forget Gideon's pitcher and his speared vision, and don't fail to remember that the Philistines were defeated by a man who dreamed that a barley loaf rolled on them, and destroyed them. Our souls are as small as the cumin seed; I often think far less in size; so we have to be misers with our knowledge, and the words we employ to frame it; otherwise, we are spendthrifts of our own bones, and thinking of you, and Sherwood Anderson, and musing, as I consider the tragedy of waste, we cannot afford to spoil the hands that sow the seeds.

Meanwhile, Jonathan, I am breaking my own poor head to pieces endeavoring to complete *Because I Was Flesh,* and though I give you all sorts of priestly advice, I don't know what to do myself. I admit with shame, shall I add, that I am also using wit to relieve tragedy, and also because I have not the bravery to complete the book that in a way is being composed by my Mother, without mining the comic veins. I must walk in comic socks or perish in buskined drama.

April 6th, 1962
Did I give you my deepest thanks for your very gifted piece on *Truth Is More Sacred;* I should also add that the first paragraph of your epistle is a fine poem. I am not being trite, and it might seem such false and easy poesy to babble this way, but it is the truth. And that

is why I have urged you to be more formal; the unusual gift you have; you can become an extremely clever versifier, coming into a glistering and rather vulgar fame in a short while, or you can pass through the dark woods as I have had to do and am still doing, and imagine that you are a cenobite and even a scorpion-like truth-sayer. In the end we die, and one might say what does it matter, but it does, and for no ontological reasons either. While we live, some of us like to do the best we can, and others the least. It all depends upon the structure of your body, whether you are to be a renowned toad and join the swarm in the universal pond or take your chances and be alone, and get as your guerdon an occasional epistle from a man who is as much of an exiled Cain as you are. I do what I do because I cannot do anything else. We are what we do, and no matter how we try to improve our natures, the results seem better but are only different.

November 9th, 1962
What people do with their privy lives is what nature, or custom, or both, or one goading and abetting the other, prompts them to do. I don't care about that; let a man make a strong male verb, a virile adverb, a sentence that is stout as the Pelian Ash, and he is utterly moral. But if I print such a remark, people will take this for a recanting, and believe I am currying favor with my unknown, invisible, and metaphysical public. Reputation bought at the price of my integrity will yield me more rubbish than I care to cast into my soul. I have enough of the garbage of Tophet there already, and I must, if I can, survive these wicked, brutal times, and not be just another scribbler of Grub-Street, who adores his pockets, and cares not a straw for others who are struggling to print their poems and their prose and their hurt and vanquished spirits.

February 23rd, 1963
I have your lovely poem, Emblems for the Little Dells, and Nooks, and Corners of Paradise. I cannot even begin to tell you how much I care for it, and that it is an infamy that you have not yet found a publisher for verse rarely seen in this century.

Not above a week ago I wrote Sir Herbert, telling him that you were too reticent to ask him to read your poetry, and that I would be most grateful to him if he would.

Be sure of my deep feeling for the Poem; I am not here referring to lines that have wondrous music in them, for the simple reason that I am tired, very. Have been working on notes, and doing a lengthy essay on Allen Tate's essays, which I have been at for many months. . . .

July 2nd, 1963

I abhor children's books. Why, aren't children human beings? We imagine they are monsters, belonging to some separate race of imbeciles, and compose verse and tales particularly for them. Why not give a boy or girl the best; he can misunderstand Blake or Herrick just as easily at 10 years of age as he can at 50. Better to misconceive the best than to understand the worst. . . .

Being a valetudinary is a great bore; though time is a human invention the days are as heavy on my head as the mountains in Africa were on the shoulders of Atlas.

July 26th, 1963

Could you, when you are ready to write again, do a longer poem; you must know that I do not measure work by its length. However, I feel that it is time that you find certain absolutes (that they are not does not matter; that you struggle for them does) and make a vision for yourself that will pervade a whole book and bind together all the ideas, feelings, and metres. Otherwise, you have a charming few stanzas on one page, then a clever or witty one on another, and though nobody could mistake the identity of the poet, there is not a strong, vehement river of emotion or wisdom coursing over the bedrock of the entire work.

November 11th, 1963

I toiled more years for a few truthful books than Jacob did in Laban's Field; in seven years you can get yourself a squint-eyed Leah, but in 14 a radiant Rachel.

January 22nd, 1964

I am delighted to hear that Paul Metcalf delivered some fine remarks about *Because I Was Flesh*. He has an oceanic imagination, and I remember, as if one could forget that great moist element, Water, his Manuscript which you are kind enough to send to me. I know of no one who has done that kind of wise reading, save him, yourself, and may I include me. If he does not compose a *boke* for Piscis some day I shall then say that the nothing I know is not even nothing.

June 27th, 1964

Can anybody give good counsel to another, or is the heart absolutely surd when advice is offered? Do you want a quick reputation, or do you propose to be a poet? That is the dilemma as I see it. Your seniors never gave you a good paradigm, but you insist on copying their mannerisms. Learning is not knowledge unless it is an inward volcano that explodes into a sonnet. You cannot use pedestrian conversation, place alongside it instructions pasted on the door of a rooming house, and add to that, a line or two from the Purgatorio. That is the modern fraud, and it makes for outside poetry which is composed in Gaza, and not on the holy hills of Jerusalem. I know I have told you this many times, and just as many times, with rare exceptions, you have shunned my exhortations. When you come to the conclusion that the Word is First after the Void has been dissolved then you will be as good as God or as weary from going to and fro in the earth as Lucifer. Should you wish to circumnavigate your soul it is not good enough just to cite Hakluyt's *Voyages;* you yourself must make the journey, and all the pelagic meadows must be within you and not added on to an easy piece of American jargon.

February 3rd, 1967
Craft Horizons arrived just this moment, and I have looked at your prose, not read it, in *The Southern Appalachians.* And it is indeed very fine, and as I have scanned lines here and there can say that without equivocation. No doubt, natural history is a source of your force. We are animals and without thinking what we should do, we go to what we need. . . .

You have my love and my friendship and the only way you can keep them is to sit down on your hunkers and wear them out until you have composed a book full of honey, hyacinth, gall, sumach, and love.

March 4th, 1967
I also stumble in the winds or grope in the darkness at my desk; the pilgrimage is not finished until nature says that it is.

II. "DOWN HERE IT IS ZERO"

November 29th, 1955
Maybe you will care for Big Sur; I care little for the tramps of arts and letters (this is not a pecuniary definition of those fancy gnomes in denims and with crew haircuts), and have been, I fear, to too many colonies of the Muses to risk another mischance. The truth is, there is nowhere to go; either you go to Philistia, and attempt to observe all the merciless cash register proprieties of the bourgeoisie, or you take up erotica, and the debilities of Henry James, and his successors, and live at Big Sur, or Provincetown, or Truro, with the malevolent Cape Codders, and the well-to-do haberdashery authors. Paris I found little to my liking; Stendhal hated the big solitudes there, and Flaubert preferred to be an eremite in Rouen than hazard his person in Montmartre. You have to go through it. I did, and though one can never weigh experience, in some ways it set me back as a writer several lustra.

January 12th, 1955
I have had four years of boreal exile here [Santa Monica], and I thirst to see some human beings. It may be that Highlands, North Carolina, is another desert. However, two or three persons can cure the bleakest locality. . . .

I have grown to fear places, finding that most of them are as deaf as the adder.

February 4th, 1958
I am caught in the middle between the marxists who I think have killed letters and the cartels who have destroyed everything, the earth, the furrow, the elms, human affections, the liver, and I think the pudendum too.

June 13th, 1958
I feel that politics has been the malignant harpy defecating upon all those repasts of our soul and mind. I don't think it is possible to create a civilization in a land that covers more territory than the body of a Titan. Small nations are best for poets and thinkers.

August 3rd, 1958
As you say, no one hears of anything in such a vast wilderness, the great mechanical forest out of which St. John the Baptist comes forth with a cruller and bottle of coca cola. I once succeeded in enduring Washington, that cement quagmire glutted with dollar tombstones called government buildings, for 10 days.

August 10th, 1958
The people who run the *Partisan Review* are a pair of oleaginous rogues. I was the original founder of the *Partisan Review,* but when the communists insisted that Rahv, Phelps or Philips join me, I left. They were so ignorant that they thought that Erskine Caldwell was culture. I knew Caldwell when he was a solitary mendicant writer who was the author of *The American Earth* which had some real quality, or I thought so at the time. I met him at a party given in honor of Mae West's autobiography. I guess everybody was there to see her straw-stuffed bosom. Edmund Wilson thought she was marvelous; I thought she was drugstore trash. Hart Crane arrived, very drunk and gracious, and got up a petition to ask her to sing Frankie and Johnnie were Lovers.

September 23rd, 1958
You must be mindful of the species of nihilism that obtains everywhere

at present. A copy of the *Daily Graphic,* as one young man asserted, is not a classic, but a foe of sensibility, human consideration for others, and a courteous heart. . . .

I am absolutely nowhere in America at the age of 58. I have been in exile in this land since I was a boy. But it is the only country I know, and homeless here I somehow or other touch the ground, a threshold, and a few people who are my kindred even if they don't recognize it.

May 5th, 1959
We cannot shun the malady of our century; that we both know. The maggots either feed on our ideas or our heart; as for the body that is hopeless. We die defeated utterly, anyway, and there is nothing between us and the tomb, at least that is our penultimate delusion, but pythagorean numbers, herbs, the grass of the second day of creation, and our work. Aristotle says that the poet loves his work best of all the craftsmen. Let us do what we can. Shun the obvious mistakes, and maybe all is not lost.

March 3rd, 1960
I just received the most enchanting epistle from Sir Herbert who lectured in Stockholm with the King of Sweden as part of his audience, and the Vikings in tails and stuffed shirts playing harps and pipes was a moiety of the whole ceremony. We are fools to have been born, my dear Jonathan, in a land that cares not one whit whether we are alive or not. Had we been parlous or had any acuity at all we would have selected one of the Scandinavian countries as our birthplace. Myself, I would rather have sat with Job on his muck-heap than be alive now.

July 22nd, 1960
I want to go to the sea, write in the morning, bathe in the afternoon.

August 6th, 1960
I have your very good and human letters, and you must imagine that I am quite coarse not to have replied at once. First, I was traveling, was in Gibraltar, Algeciras, Sevilla, Madrid, Barcelona and then Mallorca. Then, my dear Jonathan, the house was not yet completed; but now, done in the old Majorcan style, including meubles antiguas, it is finished; this in truth, my first epistle written to any one. A letter came from Sir Herbert, asking me where I was. Yes, I hope and pray ι am still extant, always a good query, since few souls ever die, and almost none ever rise from their squalid everyday graves.

December 15th, 1960
Your letters are always the manna and the quail in the small wilder-

ness of my room on Horatio Street; this is our arcadian megalopolis; these streets too were the epitaphs Melville composed as he walked in his solitudes on Little Twelfth and Gansevoort Streets, or toward Bleecker.

December 7th, 1961

I was not thriving in Spain; my brain was beaten to pieces by sun, so that I came to abhor that fiery planetary rock, and pined for headlands, dour, hard weather, marsh and fen grounds, and so I have that, and at least now can work.

January 26th, 1962

What you say of poor, maimed [William Carlos] Williams is sad and a terrible wound; what has anybody to look forward to, or to take a glance to the rear of him, past is present, and present is yesterday, and who can bear it?

March 1st, 1962

Am sorry that your trip to New York was more or less worthless. There is no place to go, and so we travel! you and I, and what for, just to imagine that we could go somewhere else, though as Zeno said there is no motion. . . .

I hope Eleanor Anderson will be pleased with my tribute to the genius of Sherwood, a fine, warm loving nature. He tried to live with the rural folk, which I could never do, for I feel that they are more malicious than the bad people in the big cities. I hate religion and virtue and anybody who feigns to be a writer, a human being, or even good for nothing; every one is just too sly and has too guileful a heart to pretend that he is anything at all; soon as a man leaves off telling you what a nobody he is, he will begin to tell you what an abstruse talent he has. No, we live in a different sort of century, and no one can afford even to say that he is honest; it's too hazardous an admission, and implies a great deal of guilt.

August 17th, 1963

Your citation from Burton is very fine, but my dear Jonathan, I have assailed men who have said perversely, I want to be alone, in several books. Do you think I live as a solitary because it pleases me, or because it is impossible to find people who are even human enough to laugh or exchange an easy platitude with you.

January 1st, 1964

If you wish to compose a truthful poem, you will have to acquire a fine and solid sodality of enemies. You have too many friends to free yourself for your own Pisgah and verse. It's not a pleasant admonition; sure, I should like to tell you that I have a hogshead of friends everywhere. When I get a letter I think it is the second or third day of creation, long after there was nothing but water and mist and emptiness in what is now supposed to be the universe.

Involuntarily I live like an eremite; whom can I talk to besides a wise book? Make no doubt about it, I enjoy chattering as much as the next fool, but when I wish to ascend the Cordilleras who is there to accompany me? Each man must go alone to his writing, to his adages, and to his grave.

January 6th, 1964
I myself have the most harmonious feelings with about 9 people, but get along with classic understanding with six hundred million Chinese I have never met, and have nothing against the Pakistanians, the Indians and the Siberians. So for a recluse I do rather well. . . . By god, Jonathan you know everybody, and that is why you are in trouble always. You've just got to fall out with someone; otherwise you would be characterless. . . .

Instead of these walking-tours you might collect a pair of geniuses, so that I won't be so lonely. You called me in isolation; though in book after book I have impugned those who feign that solitude is anything but a graveyard triumph. I see nobody because whom is there to see.

January 22nd, 1964
Never be puffed up, but consider no man your peer. Everybody I ever regarded as my equal soon made it quite clear to me that I was far less than he was. The only people who are equal to each other are the avaricious, the predatory, the vicious, and those who are for themselves.

May 6th, 1964
I intended to return to New York in August, to look for an apartment, and that is a harrowing thought. An Indian had a summer and winter dwelling; in one season he lived on the coast and in another in a hammock in the forest. We can find nothing, and imagine we are progressive.

October 9th, 1966
Let our follies be mountainous; may we breathe air no one else can, and find those eagle nests at the peaks. Down here it is zero, and often I believe I live in a world without people.

III. "SIGHS AND CONSTELLATIONS BETWEEN BOARDS"

October 4th, 1956
All intelligent Americans are extremely alone, and you are helping to dissolve those Frozen Straits in which most of us are either dying from the cold or are benumbed every day of our lives.

February 24th, 1958
I cannot tell you too often that what you are doing is valorous. Whatever is good or strong in American Literature today is virtually underground. The Mind is in the rotten contemporary Catacombs where only heretics dare pray to the Nine Daughters of the Arts and where Christ with the Ass's Head may be seen. . . .

In the past I walked the streets to get Kenneth Fearing printed, and the late Sol Funaroff, who had a generous heart, and was a communist, and myself, got out Fearing's poems. He never even thanked me. But let us say that he showed monstrous ingratitude toward his own talent, for after that he never did anything with it.

May 12th, 1958
I have genuine sympathy with Walter Lowenfels. He sends me his verse to read, and one of the poems, Giordano Bruno, I thought very fine and moving. He says that he cannot get his work published because he is a communist. I had to tell him that I cannot get my work reviewed because I am not. So everybody is killing everybody else, and the pariah of that immense mortuary cartel, AMERICA, the poet, is the sacrificial bull and the booty.

August 3rd, 1958
I never had any use for the whole Montparnasse literary crowd. In the early days I saw Robert McAlmon who was married to a lesbian, now the mate of H. D. in Lausanne. I never liked McAlmon, and I never asked him for any kindness, nor received any. However, when I learnt that he was a tubercular waif at Desert Hot Springs, the alley of Palm Springs, my wife and I used to visit him once a month. I tried to get a publisher to do something for him, but without success. The truth is that I had no faith in his work; however, he had printed Joyce, Pound, Hemingway, when they were prentices, and obscure, and, of course, he was neglected by the dead and the living. He died a year or so ago, and now some graduate student at one of the American colleges is doing a thesis on him! . . .

You help others because that is your appetite, and in the end you are likely to be as forsaken as poor McAlmon. I hope not. I have done a great deal for some of the people you mention. I helped them, and they helped them. That does not mean that I can rejoice in their isolation or in their bitterness. Every day I drink of the bitter waters of Mareh.

August 10, 1958
I think your publishing list is impressive, even if there are individual mistakes. Since the whole of life is a folly the best we can do is to commit it.

September 23rd, 1958
I would, if my suggestions do not irk you, because you know how to print and bind a book with great taste, and I don't know anything about either, bring out books that do not simper or are not eccentric. When one is a poet he does not have to try to look like one. The enemy recognizes him even in the gray, death-like double-breasted suit. All a poet nowadays has to do is to open mouth to sow dragon's teeth, and so it is not essential that he dress like one, or that you clothe a book with upside-down photographs. Let us try to be as simple and plain as we can about what we feel. Were you a parcel of that beat generation, you would not immolate your person and pocket-book in an impossibilist's effort to bring to others books. I would not go on writing either; ask yourself, what do you write for? Ask yourself all the questions that press down upon your identity so that you won't do more stupid things than I did when I was your age. We are born fools and die wretches, and there is no necessity to be more clownish or miserable than we already are.

It is good to publish those who cannot find someone to do it. You also have another task, even more significant, to print the works of those who will be of use to purblind souls. We are all Cimmerians, living in some subterranean bog in our souls, and when I glance through a volume, I don't want to know whether this author cannot otherwise find someone like yourself to bring him out. What is most important is that, whatever age he is, he can be the viaticum of my own nature, and give me enough food so that my own identity can soar for an afternoon or at least until dusk. In other words, despite the fact that it is very hard for young people, and also the older ones, to get somebody to place their sighs and constellations between boards, what is of imperial worth is what they can do for others. Otherwise, you are bringing out books by Narcissus. There is already too much self-love in the world. Don't encourage a man to love himself more than he already does. Do what you can to impress upon him the necessity of caring for somebody else. Every page is either a vision or Circe's sty. Somehow or other most of us can gather the acorns and the masts, and we in this respect are as agile as the sea-pigs around the Pillars. What everybody requires, you and I, is a book to take us back to Isis and Osiris so that we can understand this smallest of periods we attach so much importance to, our lives. If a book is not the most acute moiety of a man's valorous pursuit for ends, then it is the devil of Gadarene.

November 1st, 1958
You should not publish writers because their wives have left them, or because they won't. You cannot afford to be a social welfare worker on Mount Parnassus. It is foolish to print the garbage of the young or of the old. You owe a good vision to the commonwealth, not because the nation has done very much for you, but simply because you wish to have an honest heart which you cannot have without more self-knowledge. What we know about others is only what we know about ourselves.

You say you are too modest to approach eminent writers or poets. I am grateful that you are not presumptuous, but you are not charitable as you imagine when you fail to print what has been done, thinking that it will be republished or that it is even known. If you are to be the gifted man I think you are, there must be some visionary structure to your own life, and what you publish is you. I give you as an example of inestimable neglect: William Carlos Williams' *Kora in Hell* published in 1920, but read by the fewest of people, and since republished by the City Lights books. Why was it not done by you? It has wonderful sights and very grassy and warm perceptions. You were under the impression that the tradesmen always take care of writers who are now established. I hate the last word since we are unstable all the days of our lives.

August 4th, 1961
We are not born for ourselves alone says Cicero.

February 1st, 1962
You have my affections, and friendship, Jonathan, and heaven knows that I will do all in my power to get your poems into the sun. I could suggest some of the stygian, venal publishers, and you would more likely have a chagrin. They degrade everybody, and if they did take a sheaf of your Poems, they would drop you after one book. You need, as I have said, a publisher who will be your shield and buckler for many years.

112

June 27th, 1964

Though you have a magnificent heart, and it is a miracle that we have a Jonathan Williams to republish Anderson's *Mid-American Chants,* what is the good of illustrating them with photographs. Or one may wonder whether the verses of Anderson are not just the subtitles for the camera work. I think all this is a parcel of your perplexities. You might ask why Ben Shahn did the drawings for *The Sorrows of Priapus.* It is the same thing we are discussing. You can't get people to read, and so you prepare as a snare for them drawings or photography, hoping that after they have glanced for a delirious minute at the camera pictures or the artist's illustrations they will then be tempted to peruse the book. I don't believe that people go from one to the other. Admiring even a great oil painting by Velasquez requires the smallest amount of intellectual attention, whereas you cannot examine Plato's *Critias* without employing all your faculties. In short, we are art-crazy because we are lazy, supine, and do not care to use our minds.

March 27th, 1965

Now I think the Anderson book is monstrous, and that you have not treated me with the affection that I thought you had for me, nor with the respect you have shown for my work. Your emphasis on photography, a lazy stepmother art, is nonsensical. Both the *Mid-American Chants* and my Note are buried beneath the snows of camera-work. As for me you don't even mention my name on the cover.

April 1st, 1965

I have never been precious or bombastic with you; you dedicated a lovely poem to me and called me your mentor and teacher; well, when do I commence to instruct you? Or do we learn nothing as we decay, alas, not much, but perhaps just a tittle. But you must, as it seems, make your own mistakes and nobody can stop you either gnomes or whatever you think I am. You pilloried me for writing some trashy books; did I become perverse or angry with you? I said it was the truth. If you bow to no man no one in turn will ever heed you, and you will be another vulgarian of American Letters or just a broken, fissured man, another 50 year old boy of literature. You must decide, and *now,* later is the tomb or nothingness.

June 29th, 1966

Well, I guess you know I don't require your help to lard my renown, but what kind of friendship is this? Was I ever pompous with you? You published all sorts of squalid fools, and still do. Zukofsky is a dwarf, and Olson a refrigerated verser; I was duped by them at one time, but long since realized there was no point in drudging for Narcissi.

You have never heeded my counsel, and so what remains?

Yes, I recall when Zukofsky could not get one line published, and I toiled for him as I did for that other knave, Olson, but you never learn anything. Or as Paul has it, "You are always learning, and never coming to any knowledge."

When you cease printing dizzards who have neither erudition or love for others, we can be friends again.

July 19th, 1966

Your letter came today, and I don't care to make a great nuisance over what is finished, and does not matter to me now. Then it did, not that a plain notice of me would have larded my renown. Let us ponder this very briefly and then forget about it. You took unusual pains to give prominent attention to camera-work which is a lazy and bastard art and will never increase your wisdom or mine. In short, two of three persons involved were mentioned on the cover, and I thought that extremely unfriendly and not just.

You cannot deny I have been your friend, and have in no way been a dissembler with you. You may think I have a poor opinion of the scribblers you print because of ill-feeling. I am solely concerned with you as a poet. Some verses you have written I admire, but so long as you squander your money on prosers and poetasters how can you be much better than they. We are not more, but often less than the people we venerate. . . .

There are marvelous bookshops in England; spend your money on the ancient sages and 15th and 16th century poets. I never looked for acolytes, and you did not on any occasion hear me suggest that you read a book of mine, nor will I. We admire the Andes not when we are close to them, for then they look like a dead hump of gravel and stone, but far away from them they are prodigies to our souls and intellects. So it is wiser for you to study, and not just read, which is indolent, Chapman, Drayton, Ben Jonson, Gavin Douglas, and so on, than to be issuing pigmies.

I have been telling you this for years, and you do what you did, and so do not ripen yourself.

Please heed me, even though my counsel costs you nothing. What happened to your work on herbals? I was enthusiastic about it. Keep away from causes, whether good or ill, they will be asps to your muse, and poison you, so that you will not have the strength for your real labors.

Try to be plain; should one commit an error, don't feel you are broken to pieces, or that I, for example, would be dilated if you apologized. Now I am not really seeking that. What I am saying is that what falls out of your mouth should be urned in your heart. Nothing else.

December 28th, 1966

I thought since you hid my Introduction to Sherwood Anderson that I ought to call you J. Summer, Inspector General of our Mt. Ida molehill. Jonathan Engineer, or Hercules the boy who sweeps the dung into the Augean Stables fast as I can clean it out. No matter; you won't change. I send you the 4 letter word, love: be sure to publish it.

April 18th, 1967

Could a covenant be made between two friends, you and I, I would propose that if you or I do anything at all that is unkind to the other, he should utter his whole remorse for doing it, and I believe I could keep my part of the bargain, nor am I suggesting you could not, not at all. So let us forget what has been done amiss, and I don't think we have harmed each other, or that that has been our endeavor; you just had a real fainting spell over the joys of the mechanical camera. Never forget: In the beginning was the Word, and the Word became flesh, and after that came the devil of Gadarene, the printing press, the auto, the airplane, the super-market and the bauble called the Camera.

You have my love, and know I am your devoted friend, because I have only one evidence as proof of it, I always was.

THOMAS MEYER: *Invoke the healers and let the*
cures commence

A translation for Edward Dahlberg from the Old English version of a Salernitan text (ca. 1100) beginning: *Incipit liber qui peri didaxeon . . .*

Which is the revelation of how the learned leeches wisely investigated and verified the leechcraft hidden for many years. The first were Apollo, his son Aesculapius, Hippokrates, and his uncle Asklepios. These four invented the earliest system of leechcrafts. About one thousand and five hundred winters after Noah's flood, in the days of Artaxerxes, king of Persia, they lit the lamp of healing arts. We know that Apollo first invented *methods,* the iron knives one heals with; Aesculapius *empirics,* the cures of healing; Asklepios *logics,* the cup of keeping the law; and Hippokrates, *theories,* the contemplation of sickness.

Then Plato and Aristotle, the very wise philosophers, followed these leeches and said man's body like the rainbow had four humours: the liquid in the head; the blood in the breast; the raw gall in the innards; and the dark gall in the bladder. Each one of them rules for three months: from the 18th of January to the 8th of April the head's humours wax; from the 18th of April to the 8th of July the blood in the breast waxes; from the 18th of July to the 8th of October the raw gall waxes in the innards, hence these days are called *cynades,* that is the *dies caniculares* of which there are five and forty. During those days no leech can properly help any sick man. And the fourth section is from the 18th of October to the 8th of January when the black gall of the bladder waxes.

These things are revealed according to the cardinal points of heaven, earth, air, and the deepness. So man was set as the Lord pleased. These things demand meditation and method.

GUY DAVENPORT

American history is discontinuous and without a memory. At any given time it can contain only a few select icons to the exclusion of

117

PHOTO BY JONATHAN WILLIAMS, CIRCA 1958.

all others. God is dead, say the mooncalves dancing from the seminaries, fun people who could come all over the tic douloureux and micturitional were they to meet the cinder-eyed Herr Nietzsche himself. They never say that the God of Habakkuk is dead. They have never heard of Him. Nor looked into Habakkuk to find Him there. The American past, most of the present, and all of the future is kept in storerooms, and our culture is a well-kept secret among a few technicians. Even the technicians aren't aware of each other. If a man works in a disjunct mode it goes hard with him. If, as Edward Dahlberg does, he has Alexandrian rhetoric in his head, and has dreamed in gaudy barbershops of the yellow Scamander curling through timothy and asphodel, what is the present Late Victorian giggle to do with him? If he deals in Dreiser's and Anderson's world of high vulgarity and broken hearts and has well dined often with Sir Thomas Browne and has thought much with Roderick Usher upon the old African satyrs and Aigipans in Pomponius Mela, who is surprised that he makes college professors cough and enthusiasts strain the harder to fake a response? The spittoons and pointed shoes, the Missouri sun, the utter weariness of Priapos in a world of TV and drugstores—we shall get around to that, in time; the whore Publicity bides her time. But what are we to do with these dialogues with Sir Herbert Read, with this urbanity and learning and polish? From Cotton Mather to Edward Dahlberg, who has quoted Diodorus Siculus at us? Opsimaths and bluenoses have said that our best literature is half trash, if not all, but they have cried out in fear and stupidity; Dahlberg does it in cold blood and with bewildering authority.

He is that most difficult of things to be in the United States, a man of feeling. Nor is he sweet or compromising or hypocritical: the secondary modes we most frequently use to run interference for any sensitivity whatsoever. In a world that counts more the manners with which a thing is said than the sentiment or fact itself, he is gloriously boorish, like an Arab sheyk at a Unitarian service. He is earthy and overcivilized all at once, smooth and bristly by uncalculable turns, and wildly melancholy at all times. We do not know what to think of such an Habbakuk; he does not play the game. Politics, religion, fads, movements, groups, styles, editorial boards: they have all failed to touch him. Like all stubbornly personal men he seems fetched on, decidedly curious and unaccountably outlandish. Never mind. He is there, like Doughty and Zukofsky and Pumpelly and Jardiel Poncela. There are, there shall always be, men thankful for his genius and the labors to which he put it.

JOSEPHINE HERBST

I don't think Edward Dahlberg needs homage so much as he needs readers. Many, not a few; not even "the happy few." To expect that is probably to ask more than he may get in his lifetime, but I would bet that *Because I Was Flesh* will have a long life after we are all gone. Dahlberg's vision of the world is tragic. His pessimism is an absolute. But the man who has a tragic vision both accepts the world and rejects it. He accepts it in the sense that he devotes himself to understanding it, lives in it, speaks his mind about it, and does not withdraw from it. He rejects it in the sense that its occupations and values cannot satisfy him. His hatred of contemporary "reality" is intimately bound up with an inherent pessimism, and pessimism in turn is one of the prime conditions of his ceaseless quest for ideal forms. Perhaps too much is made of his "style." Style may not save us but it is a force. In Dahlberg's case, it is so intimately connected with what he says, and what he says is so much a part of his modernity, that it is a mistake, it seems to me, to carry admiration of his style to extremes. In doing so, the substance somehow gets bypassed. As a penetrating and implacable observer of himself and others, Edward Dahlberg has tried to look beyond the vanities and the vices at the fears which give birth to them and to be less impressed by the sensuality, cruelty, and cowardice of men than by their illusions, their sense of being lost in a world not understood by them. This is an essential part of his modernity. It works within assumptions that are of the twentieth century: the fragmented immediacy of experience, the constant fading or alteration of forms, the oppressive heterogeneity of phenomena. Edward may castigate the human species for its restlessness but he knows that man would not be restless and anxious were he not seeking knowledge and some sort of spiritual haven. Because he takes himself with desperate seriousness, everything he writes is a work of self-discovery. But the self he goes after is not isolated in a vacuous rummage room. His rejection of contemporary reality may have sharpened the collector's urge for echoes and symbols but it has also given him a documentary interest in *things* for what they can tell of the imagination. Things are corrupted or corrupting. He is tortured by the fact that mind has been turned into matter, the ideal converted into ludicrous and detestable paraphernalia, but the subject is always the imagination and often of the orgiastic kind.

There is so much that is paradoxical, quixotic, contrary about Edward Dahlberg that it is impossible to sum him up and pack him away in a convenient nutshell. Is it possible always to agree with him? Or to share his exclusive literary tastes? But there is consistency even in his inconsistency; he is always provocative. What writer is less afraid of absurdities or willing to show himself as ridiculous? If only because he falls below his own nature, contrasting what he aspires to be with what he is; his nature is to aspire even when he may cease to hope. Perhaps his faith is an allegiance to something which to him is superior to the world and yet never to be achieved in it. His fate is to see the world too clearly to accept its values. It is the combination of colliding, tempestuous elements that makes the ideas born of this vision so moving in their sobriety and truthfulness.

JOHN WAIN

"But to subsist in bones, and be but Pyramidally extant is a fallacy in duration. Vain ashes, which in the oblivion of names, persons, times, and sexes, have found unto themselves, a fruitlesse continuation, and only arise unto late posterity, as Emblemes of mortall vanities; Antidotes against pride, vainglory, and madding vices.

120

Pagan vainglories which thought the world might last forever, had encouragement for ambition, and finding no *Atropos* unto the immortality of their Names, were never dampt with the necessity of oblivion. Even old ambitions had the advantage of ours, who acting early, and before the probable Meridian of time, have by this time found great accomplishment of their designes, whereby the ancient *Heroes* have already out-lasted their Monuments, and Mechanicall preservations. But in this latter Scene of time we cannot expect such Mummies unto our memories, when ambition may fear the Prophecy of *Elias,* and *Charles* the fifth can never hope to live within two *Methusela's* of *Hector.*"

"The Greek doctors of *materia medica* paid as much heed to seminal visions as to the cure of elephantiasis, leprosy or poltfoot. The plant called Nymphaea, used in a medicinal beverage, was drunk by persons who cohabitated in their sleep with Aspasia or Helen of Troy.

"We know less about amours than the bramble frog: the absence of elms, alders, willows and the vitex, or even marshes, bogs, rivers and brooks in our cities has produced every imaginable deformity: impostumes, senility, short groins, groveling bums, sniveling ballocks and a simpering anus. What we do not inherit we catch from fools, and stupidity is more contagious than the pox. We should know in what months it is best to be continent; the matrons, during the Greek Thesmophoriazûsae, strewed their beds with the vitex, not unlike the willow, observing at that time the strictest chastity."

The first of those passages is from Sir Thomas Browne, the second from Edward Dahlberg. I put them side by side not because Dahlberg is in any way a mere imitator of Browne (as Charles Lamb, for instance, was so often fatally tempted to be), but to indicate the kind of pleasure I get from reading him. Obviously Edward Dahlberg is aware of the English seventeenth century, of Browne and Traherne and the King James Bible; but mention of the Bible recalls us to the fact that the writers of that time were duly impressed and influenced by this Colossus that had appeared in their midst, that the rhythms of this great period of our prose were haunted by the rhythms of the Bible, and that the Old Testament, being translated from the Hebrew, carried over some of the features of Hebrew poetry and inspired writing generally: the wavelike rhythms, the stately repetitions, the habit of parallelism which enjoins that a key statement is made twice in slightly different form. If Dahlberg is nourished by the English seventeenth century in prose, as Eliot was nourished by it in verse, one of the reasons is that all fertility is a circular process; life sinks into the soil and rises again; what those far-off ancient Jews gave to us via the Bible, Dahlberg is able to use via seventeenth-century English; he gives the new push that sends all that life flowing onward, like blood being pumped by the heart.

Then there is so much more, all his own and all traditional. Rhetorical farce, the extravagant use of cunningly deployed absurdity, as in the delicious phrase "sniveling ballocks and a simpering anus," is a trademark of Dahlberg's; it is never far away even in his most poignant passages. So that the reader is continually either moved to tears or convulsed with laughter. To read a book like *Because I Was Flesh* is like reading half a dozen ordinary books at the same time. Scorn, tenderness, lyrical ebullience, wisdom, infinite sadness, and underneath all, like an unnoticed subterranean stream, the irrepressible self-mockery of the Jew. There is no writer quite like Edward Dahlberg. May he write many more books for our delight, and may he be aware of our gratitude and our homage.

ALLEN TATE

I have been told that Edward Dahlberg is the kind of writer I should not like, being the kind of writer (whatever kind that is) I am. I not only like him; I think he is the most important writer to come into prominence since the Second World War. (He was known to a few in the Twenties and Thirties.) I will not list his triumphs. Let it be enough to say that *Because I Was Flesh* is a masterpiece of autobiography which tells us more about the United States, in its alienated and rejected side, than any other book of the century.

The brutal honesty—kept at an aesthetic distance through historical perspective—is delivered to the reader in all the arts and wiles of a master of fiction.

PAUL METCALF

In Kansas, when a man got ahead, made some money, he sent his son East to Harvard (the little boys in Dahlberg's orphan asylum sang "We'll fight for the name of Harvard")

and there it is, the schizoid split, so American, so middlewestern: the mean, grimy things we do to make money—and the "culture," the unreal world of knowledge, the reward of it all

in no writer, in the past, has the split been more evident and perplexing than in Dahlberg: thrusts into his sordid Kansas background, alternating with heaped-up Greek, Egyptian, Hebrew allusion—"several thousand volumes are the making of a marvelous mask"

But in *Because I Was Flesh,* the two mountains grind, finally, together, and the disturbance is at least seismic—there is new wit, there is personal honesty, the scalpel has been honed, sharp as one of Lizzie's razors—Mother and Son are relentless, slicing, driving to the end of the book

all of Dahlberg's earlier work appears now to have been the manufacture and trial run of materials: he has put them together, at last, in this work

and we are shaken

KARL SHAPIRO

One must risk the psychological vulgarism of "explaining" Dahlberg, although he is the best explainer of himself. In a letter to Herbert Read dated 1955, as a sauce to the attack on Joyce, he

123

raises the problem of "the failure of the Father in our literature; Zeus, Osiris, Apis, Serapis, no longer honor the anti-heroes of our imaginative works, and the authors are lickerish and scatological, instead of carnal, mythopoeic, and virile."

The absence or nonexistence of Dahlberg's own father is magnificently wailed in his autobiography. And who is to say that the orphan and illegitimate has not a primal vision as artist. In the end, complaints against Dahlberg seem trivial and ineluctable, for his sorrows mass into a shadow of nobility which silences criticism. His petulance and misunderstanding of the Modern are one thing; his disgust for the necessarily disgusting of modern art and literature must be brushed aside; but his blind loyalty to himself as poet, prophet, and *l'inconnu*—these are his birthright, by all means. No one in his right mind could envy him, except a poet.

HUGH KENNER

"My life was now so hopeless that I wrote a book": that's the Dahlberg tone, of which "Jewish fiction" is the commercialized caricature. For Dahlberg means each of his words; moreover he isn't proffering himself, a sham-existential court dwarf, for our amusement. Though the intensely personal guarantees every line, he won't play a role or project a character. Hence the purity of his cry, like Melville's. It recalls Lawrence's answering cry, Lawrence's which is the evoked response to so much of American literature. "There are five trash towns in greater New York, five garbage heaps of Tofeth. A foul, thick wafer of iron and cement covers primeval America, beneath which cry the ghosts of the crane, the mallard, the gray and white brants, the elk and the fallow deer. A broken obelisk at Crocodopolis has stood in one position for thousands of years, but the United States is a transient Golgotha." That's the voice of an obliterated landscape, not of a hired Jeremiah.

124

IHAB HASSAN

In the end, criticism can only praise.

Here is Edward Dahlberg, master of metamorphoses. See him don the Helmet of Mambrino and wrap about him the Mantle of Elijah? Now he dances naked like Priapus. Now he wails like the Man of Sorrows. Always, he wanders—solitary, banished from Abraham's bosom. Hera, Isis, and Astarte look on his fate; parched Tammuz and bloody Quetzalcoatl know his name.

Thus the cadences of Dahlberg's prose rise and fall, awakening the heroes of Israel, Hellas, and Rome; the pagan Earth winks at the sound of "gibing Pilate" and slumbers again. Dahlberg is a writer, and this is what the writer says: "he who fawns upon Muses is more difficult to grasp than Proteus." The forms of art take flesh from the mind; the forms flee.

Let us learn the lesson of Ovid in *The Metamorphoses*. Daphne turns into the virginal laurel, and Philomela, raped, into a nightingale. All shapes move into another shape. The constant is life which we call also Desire. Creation is the masterwork of Eros, and its form is Change.

"Every confusion comes from Eros," Dahlberg cries. Here truth wears a mask. Behold confusion with original eyes: behold the invisible labor of the gods. All the orisons of Dahlberg are sounds in the air but for this secret which he struggles to conceal from himself. His work is the myth of forms, fusion and confusion, history and dream, the soul and nature, man and woman, struggling to be many and one. Dahlberg is a master of metamorphoses.

Is this not art enough? Who knows what Art may be! It may prove the secret of form and change.

FRANK MACSHANE

A few years ago, Sir Herbert Read compared Edward Dahlberg to Samuel Beckett, and suggested that while both men had exceptional talent and individuality, they were somewhat outside of the mainstream of literature in English. How correct this judgment is will not be known for a century or more; in the meantime, we, his contemporaries who admire his work, can testify to what we think Edward Dahlberg has accomplished as a writer. A lonely figure, at times as insistent as Coleridge's Ancient Mariner, Dahlberg recognizes that we are all *isolatos:* his sentences and paragraphs echo and reecho this proud lament. D. H. Lawrence, who first introduced Dahlberg to the world, believed that friendship was impossible between men and women; Dahlberg has celebrated this rueful condition in book after book. His achievement is that he has evolved a style supple enough to construct lasting parables on Pascal's theme, that "Tous nos malheurs viennent de ne pas être seuls."

FRED MORAMARCO

For a while, Edward Dahlberg had two identities in my mind. There was the proletarian naturalist of *Bottom Dogs* and *From Flushing to Calvary,* and the enigmatic mythographer, literary critic, aphorist, and prophet of the later works. I have since read and reread all of Dahlberg's published works, and have changed my mind about the two identities. For it now seems to me that there is an essential continuity and unity to the Dahlberg canon that may be initially obscured by the *stylistic* change that occurred in his work following the publication of *Those Who Perish.* Despite Dahlberg's own disclaimers of his earlier work, and despite their surface naturalism, these novels today strike me as affecting and powerful *humanistic* documents.

Unless I am far off the mark, this is very much the central message of the later work as well. "Our poets, communal soothsayers," Dahlberg writes in *Can These Bones Live,* "abjured the speech, hunger, and blood, without which ideals and absolutes cannot be imagined." And he concludes that remarkable work, which surely should be required reading for any serious student of American

126

Literature—perhaps any literature—with the plea, "O, let man laugh the *gods* out of this world so that the heart can live in it!"

In light of this last statement, Dahlberg's preoccupation with myth, legend, and ritual may seem paradoxical, but in the revivification of myth he has found the continuum of the *human* experience—those universal concerns which link man with his fellowman and with his past. Myths enable us to "find the river back to our own identities," he writes in a letter to Isabella Gardner.

In an age of analytical criticism, the idea of a functional literature may smack too much of moralism to suit our aesthetically preoccupied tastes, but perhaps we might consider the possibility that we have been spending far too much time on "dead grammar criticism," as Dahlberg calls it, and not enough time becoming cognizant of what literature reveals to us about our lives. Having made this transition, we might be better able to appreciate the essential wisdom of Dahlberg's position as stated in a recent interview: ". . . if a book does not help you to discover yourself and to make you a more fervent person than you were before you read it, then we can say that the book is dross. . . . We have produced many cold books, but I don't think that people should be more refrigerated than they already are. If after reading a book they do not have more tropical livers than they had, the book has not only been useless, but an evil."

HAROLD BILLINGS

The reader of Dahlberg's tragedy is a participant in its visionary suffering and triumph. Man would long ago have been buried by his own sensibility had he no prophet, priest, or poet to free him. Ritual, prayer, and poetry save us. The poet assumes a cross under which any man might tremble. Dahlberg realizes this when he calls Shakespeare the Christ of literature. And Dahlberg bears the blessing and the burden of his own amazing voice. His sorrow is a song for the reader who cannot sing.

There is a dream of Jesus in *Because I Was Flesh*. And how

much more of the book is real, and how much dream, makes little difference. The historical reality of Edward Dahlberg is no more important than that of Christ. For as Dahlberg says, ". . . the only real history is the mythical one. Soon as a man dies he is a legend. Man must eat fables, or starve his soul to death."

American literature, full as it is of rationalism and naturalism, is poor soil for fable. It is Edward Dahlberg's distinction that he has grown parables in this earth.

KIM TAYLOR

Designing a book for a writer in some measure supposes a shedding of one's own skin, the assumption of another's. Not knowing the man Dahlberg, I sought him in the manner of his prose and so grew a fiery beard, drew over my whitened head a robe of rough hemp, wore a raven on my shoulder. "I derive from the Old Testament," Dahlberg wrote to me once in a confirmation of my guise. To match his poetry, then, I sewed my heart to my sleeve, put on cardboard sandals, and made willing to walk upon the scarlet coals. "I am a tender misanthrope," he wrote again, "that is, a man who says he distrusts everyone because he has been deceived so often, but who finds it absolutely essential to his nature to be duped again."

Any failure of the design must seem a failure of identification with one so alien and apart. I do not know why he cannot permit himself the peace he has so well earned, but his words sound like a roll of thunder over the literary garden parties, bringing refreshment to those who do not run from the dark rain of his prose and his pronouncements.

The stylists are few. Raw words find most reward, and they may come without check or subjection to craft, without care or cease or silence. Dahlberg, as one of the ancients, speaks with a slow, ancestral voice; at some cost to him it seems, his words issue out of silence and point to it. Words lie like leaves in still warm coverts, among roots, in windless places, but the heart in flight or fallen low is all as silent as Icarus now.

ROBERT KELLY

> *My spirit is not huffed up with fat fume*
> *Of slimy ale, nor Bacchus' heating grape.*
> *My mind disdains the dungy muddy scum*
> *Of abject thoughts, & envy's raging hate.*
> *True judgement slight regards opinion;*
> *A sprightly wit disdains Detraction.*

Sprightly. Romantic & Puritan are the two faces of Will. With barebones sprezzatura, a merry Aristotle sports among chaste marbles, disdains the dungy muddy scum of abject (= low, vulgarized by arithmetic, spread thin and sleazy) thoughts. Marston's words precisely shade it; Dahlberg is lifted up from (& thus, by the coherency of things, *by*) what he most disdains. His is the power of lyric rejection; a dismayed intellect looks in at a world truant fingers itch to grapple.

I don't know how to say about Edward Dahlberg. I've read him since I was 15 & have never felt the need to place him in a system or cope with his presence in any way other than reading. He turns me on. He excites me to acts of rhetoric & intellect; he frightens me with a morality grounded in the irritability of living tissue. The wisdom of the *tigers of wrath* feeds on the energy of their own flesh. He seems endlessly fascinated by skin, despises the "grand simplifications" of politics or religion that distract us from the ache & triumph of skin. Is it Mediterranean, that peasant sense of a man's magnificence or utterance undercut by bleeding piles or scabies?

A cleansing happens. As the victorian chimneysweep gave even his globed manhood into the cleansing anguish imposed on him by a surfeited society, Dahlberg confronts our own stuffed, divided world & will not please us with the easy drama of the passions. He cries *sweep* or '*weep* & will not tell us love stories. Fabula amatoria is church latin for novel; we do well to remember that, the novel is love-story, a shunned form to those who will not tell one. Conspicuous is Dahlberg's struggle to inaugurate new forms of say

& that for me rides out far beyond even the delight of his rich prose,

129

that he *will* inform us
anew, instruct us with the possibilities of form

(as in my own ado-
lescence *The Flea of Sodom* opened the gates of constructive order,
& as early as any other book told me of the shapes of telling)

For
the sake of form Dahlberg has armed himself with the strength &
nuisance of a style. He dared to enterprise with language, was not
content with the textus receptus of common usage. God knows
there are strange perils here; that antiquarianism second nature to
americans (allowing Melville, say, to fill his mouth with all the
goofy splender of the Jacobeans); the feral thicket or bowge a man
can rut himself in of his own good habits even, & vanish ever
after beneath the artifice of his style.

Dahlberg comes through,
doesn't dwindle. For all his closeness with books of an earlier
rhetoric, his ears are open, can hear through the rattle of time &
indifference the coherent music of our language. Though I do not
know if it is his purpose to vilify Time, it is Time that seems the
victim of his best success. Dahlberg will not let Time take away
our possibilities, or focus them alone in some few fashionable
glasses. Through all his antiquarianism, he operates to free us from
habit.

It is only at first sight that america comes so clearly through
all Dahlberg's rhetorical preoccupations. Is it Nashe with his nose
in the kennel or Marlowe with his mind on Ovid who keeps the
truest reverberation of that time? America continues that unlikely
land best seen out of the corner of the eye, while the imperfect
fovea busies itself frontally with rethorike or magic or whaling or
usura or Crazy Horse.

No more lies the chimneysweep of woolen
hand prone to our filth, upright in our unrightwise chimneys. Dahlberg would somewhat strip us & somewhat punish our inele-
gancies. We eat the raucous crow he flies our way. No writer since
Aquinas has distinguished so clearly appetite from appetency, &
found in the habitual prurience of the latter one clear term in

130

the degradation of Vision & the social order. The skin craves, achieves, is surfeited, suffers pain. And in a marvelous way Dahlberg's prose mimics such sensuous integument, as a small animal participates itself within the colors & textures of its landscape, perhaps (as Caillois suggests) for no other reason than the joy flesh takes in shaping & guising.

And this is where Dahlberg defeats that demon of discutability that infects our schools & measures each work of art by the amount of talk it gives rise to; I am talking, not about Dahlberg, but from Dahlberg, assessing some of the senses & convictions I find myself possessed of after some years of reading him; illegitimate to insist that he would have it that way. Like the works of Browne & Burton & Rabelais, his books baffle any critical presumption beyond explication of names & learned words, & return us to themselves where, with Dahlberg's dark genius, we find the rare world of the sensuous intellect & the instructed will.

ARNOLD GASSAN

It is strange that, being an enthusiast, I don't tell many people about Edward Dahlberg. Because I cannot paraphrase him, for one thing. Because they, those casual people passing through our lives, do not wish to know him, for another thing. Meeting his words head on after a night of television hurts. In this lonely time, when quiet and real speech are both rare, I am pleased to join this company which cheers him. Dahlberg writes words which precipitate thoughts we have sensed, or else he would not mean so much to us.

After I first encountered *The Sorrows of Priapus,* I found myself remembering two experiences I had held fast to, not understanding but hoping I might learn to understand. Both were senseless deaths. Something which Dahlberg does not speak about directly, but which is, to me, a central concern of his work. That is, that we do not die without somehow having spoken to another in a way which lets him truly understand us, and thus remember us.

131

An Alaskan brown bear died in the south, near Palmer, in the spring. He was trapped unwittingly, led by his nose to the bait set for a wolf. The trapper who was my guide and I found him shortly after the trap was sprung. There was nothing to do but kill him. The trapper took careful aim, shot, and the bullet caught him in the head. But he did not die. He fell, unconscious, then after a while struggled up again, mumbling in a guttural way that seemed almost understandable.

My grandfather, a silent man, outlived his dreadful wife, then lived alone. The morning his last breath was left to him he walked to the neighbors', quietly accepted his coffee, and then fell asleep in their chair near the table. At his bed that night I was dumbfounded at the beauty which death had revealed, and the strength, and the silence he had left me.

Neither bear nor man was able to speak to me in any language I could record, or translate. It is my failure, I suspect. Yet on reading Dahlberg, I felt that in a way these experiences, these other beings, had been given voice. The toughness of Dahlberg's cadences relates to the cogent lives of a bear and forebear which become solid, memorable examples of endurance.

I have an image in my mind of the bear who died so hard, rooting through the spring blossoms of the Alaskan muskeg. And another of my grandfather sternly and quietly refusing the surgeon's knife because the time gained was not worth the loss of privacy. And an image of Dahlberg, whom I never met except through his books, giving form to a personal tongue, a private speech, which is yet public and meaningful. This last, a creature society has tried to ignore, who yet offers the fruit of his personal search, aromatic, arcane, nourishing, necessary.

PAUL CARROLL

Somewhat burned-out paragraph about Edward
Is there any author living who is even in the same country as

Edward Dahlberg in the moral grandeur and violence of his writings? He is the Job of American Letters.

AUGUST DERLETH

Nobody speaks so well for Edward Dahlberg as Edward Dahlberg himself. His kind of honesty is unhappily far too rare in any time, but most especially in our own. He has never hidden behind any mask, he has always been completely himself, and in prose that is richer than almost any other to be found—in America or elsewhere. He is as much a genius as anyone of whom I can think, past or present, and he is consistently in the core tradition of American literature. . . . The world is seldom ready to extend genius a helping hand, but only to salute genius when he who possessed it is safely underground.

HAROLD ROSENBERG

The Dahlbergian stance puts on notice those in whom nobility, style, persistence, and other similarly arbitrary qualities are lacking that, however correct and useful their ideas, they belong to some other profession than literature.

NORMAN HOLMES PEARSON

Dahlberg is a self-made Monadnock, worth the climb, from whose summit the range of ordinary opinion seems flatter than ever.

IRVING ROSENTHAL

How many hours I have spent, days and weeks, tooling sentences from his models, trying to achieve the sudden magical turn of phrase in mid-air, or the wrung conceit, and how many times I have given up all hope, deciding that if it could be done in English, it could be done only by him! And style is not all he taught me. He was the only writer not of my generation who ever bothered to take me in hand, preach to me about the classics I had ignored, feed me with personal reminiscences of Crane, Lawrence, Ford, and so on—in short give me any identification as a writer or any sense of continuing a tradition. And that is not all. When I was finally harassed out of Morocco by the Tangier fuzz, who had just beaten a friend of mine to death, and had been trying to pin the same bogus-money rap on me, and I had no place in the world to go, and no money to get there, counterfeit or real, Edward graciously and swiftly invited me to stay at his house in Sóller de Mallorca, and that is where I wrote "Second Coming."

SID CHAPLIN

Nobody up here in Newcastle had *Because I Was Flesh*. The bookseller couldn't trace it. Finally, I asked my agents to try Methuens direct, and at long last a copy arrived.

By which time the doctors had found me six months gone with diabetes, and I was packed into hospital. I found much solace in the old, wise man: "There is no doctrine worth a straw so long as man has a pair of ballocks and a fundament." And a bloodstream that can race you into sweet perdition or, given too much sugar, of raging thirst, pellmell emaciation, and leaden eyelids. All the same, it was better to read the better I got. The man has read everything and remembers all sights, sounds, smells, and touches. If he has met a ghost then he alone of all men is capable of sketching the quick of the incorporeal. I find myself retarded when he says "Until my seventeenth year . . . I was suffering locality rather than person." At fifty the disease is at my bones, but I never knew it until this man told me.

I reckon the mother is consummated in the son. What she sought all her weary life she brought forth as an unfathered brat. . . . Do me a favor, please. Let me know the other titles.

134

CID CORMAN

I am never sure there is any tribute that we can offer anyone; surely flattery isn't tribute. I wrote to Edward Dahlberg first because his *Can These Bones Live* moved me to. And the second of the wooing of his old mother by the old man will touch and amuse and be true for generations. If he did nothing else, that would be enough. That he has evoked constantly for us, in English, part of the great heritage given us needs saying. The tribute is his own work, just as it should be, and more would be less.

Or the added words of Montaigne, which are too precise and clear to be "extra":

> **We are men and hold one to another only through our word.**
>
> **If it fails us, it destroys all our relation and dissolves all the bonds of our society.**

DOUGLAS WOOLF

To who is concerned:

At the dead end of 1964 I had stopped writing forever, and almost reading. At that time I happened upon *Because I Was Flesh,* which taught me to read again. Soon later I was writing like a freed man again. What more can one say? (This is not an excerpt, not a blurb, not a commercial, it's a letter.) With thanks.

"LORD, WE DIE ALL DAY LONG, AND COME CLOSER TO THE GRAVE
EACH TIME WE HAVE AN EXPERIENCE." FOR EDWARD DAHLBERG.
PHOTO BY NICHOLAS DEAN, 1967.

THOMAS MERTON: *Ceremony for Edward Dahlberg*

On this flashing afternoon of Ascension Thursday let me sit
  in my forest shade to praise a man of excellent language

Profuse and bushy is the eloquence of this Classic person, his
  talk is juiced with myth and with the lore of fathers who knew
  better than we

He makes all ears ring with the clamor of Romans we prefer to
  forget

What has he not done for us? Like Montaigne, Cervantes,
  Rabelais, he has dared unstop the more robust insanities of
  language

To ring changes on the hard metal of words and improve them
  with alchemy

To the drums of Cicero and Renaissance strings he has led forth
  in solemn procession dancing heroes that seem at first familiar

They summon one another in helmets and kilts from shadows of
  memory where there are no rigors but those of the dream

In which they remain lawless mummers of the unspoken

Teachers of no other sequences than those of invention

Who at once insult and charm the curious mind, disarming it with
  legitimate surprise

He writes of Kansas City as of fifteenth-century Bruges

He has the eye and pencils of Breughel or Bosch, the tongue of
  Thomas Browne, and sings the barbershops as Browne sang
  urn burial

Because he owns round words and rugous periods, experiences the
  secret rigors of medieval physicians

For whom blood and urine were not yet abstractions

138

And his busy fires are stoked at the imaginative Etna of the groin

When weary of the bickering of clerics and new lay-pontiffs, I am
    glad of his harmonies

St. François Rabelais, pray for him!

PHOTO BY AARON SISKIND.
"HOMAGE TO EDWARD DAHLBERG, ROME HIEROGLYPH, 1963."

EDWIN SEAVER

Although I don't care for *Festschrifts,* perhaps because the word is German and I am prejudiced that way, after all there's no reason a man shouldn't enjoy—or detest—his monument while he's still among the living. What little bit of clay can I contribute to a monument to Edward Dahlberg, especially when I would wish it not to be of clay but the imperishable stuff dreams are made of? Dahlberg is of my generation, even if he is a few months younger, and nobody of that generation has written so nobly or said so well what needs to be said by every writer of every generation—and usually isn't. He's a dedicated, a committed man, and in this he has what most of his contemporaries lack, not to mention a mind, a capacity for passion, and reverence for life. If he has defects, as some reviewers delight in stating in their quick perception of the obvious—straining after a gnat and missing the elephant—who hasn't? Dahlberg's greatness is that he acknowledges his mortality, and suffering transforms the human situation. If I say his *Because I Was Flesh* is one of the best books of our time, he will say: what's the other one? How are you going to erect a monument to a man like that? Besides, he comes of a people who are supposed to abhor idolatry. As I do. He has our affection, which is all he has ever asked, really. Posterity will take care of his fame.

VICTOR WEYBRIGHT

Edward Dahlberg is undoubtedly the finest writer of our time, and certainly the wisest Man of Letters in America. His candor has alienated some of his best friends and most flattering critics, but why should he care? He will be known and read when they are dust and cinders. His publishers, including me, will be forgotten—but Dahlberg will be read and quoted for generations by those who love wisdom, words, and poesy.

THEODORE WILENTZ: *for Edward Dahlberg*

Not knowing Edward Dahlberg but meeting him, you would feel that here was a gentleman, a scholar, a writer. "Style is the Man," he says, and he carries the proof with him. A gentleman, you discover, is not always a gentle man and Mr. Dahlberg is fierce in his defense of truth so that even friends are chary of loose or accommodating statements in his presence. A scholar, you learn, is not necessarily an academician and indeed Edward D. may make you wonder if the terms are not contradictory rather than synonymous. A writer, you realize, is always a dedicated man and this dominating fact must be comprehended before you can understand Edward Dahlberg, who is a high priest with a true "calling."

JAMES LAUGHLIN

Edward Dahlberg, bard and seer, is unique among American writers, one of the most extraordinary figures which our now disintegrating culture has produced. If enough people would read him, and would heed him, our culture still might be restored. His best prose will stand with the finest in the English language; sonorous and melodious, majestic in its architecture, it is noble utterance.

COBURN BRITTON: *A publisher's note to Edward Dahlberg*

Edward Dahlberg, what you say soars—
whether sour rebuke or sweet remembering,
some sad significance or sure savoring.
Disgruntlement's belied by the passionate life
of your lordly language wrought with what
real muses taught you, those real myths that
were your meals. Wit, rage, remorse and rapture
are all your argentcies, although they've brought
you precious little gold. It's an old favor
I ask—please but take but just this bit of print
from one who prints, O proudly! you.

141

KEITH WILSON: *The day of the rabbit*
(*Cambray, New Mexico, 1936, for Edward Dahlberg*)

One Sunday, they rounded us kids up,
promising a picnic and loaded us into pickups;
chattering we rode through the dust, screaming
with joy at the bumps, any high fly through the air.

At the ranch all was nearly ready:
a huge beef turned & smoked on the spit,
pickles in barrels, beans in great clay pots,
red chilis crumpled into jagged flakes
and dropped into the bubbling brown sauce.
Dutch-oven biscuits, hot & steaming,
being sampled by the cook.

The pickhandles were piled just beyond.
Each of us was given one, the details explained
by the potbellied rancher: we were to form
a huge circle, about two feet apart.
The men would join us, then we would close.

Later, moving slowly through the grass,
we scared up several rattlesnakes, various
small rats, a bird or two. The dust closed
on a tight pen in the center and there they
were: over a hundred rabbits, cottontails
& big Jacks milling, trying to break free.

Then the rancher took a pickhandle from one
of the boys and, laughing softly, walked to
the pen and hit one of the rabbits, breaking
his back. The rabbit screamed high & shrill,
went on screaming, he hit another & another,
soon all the boys were in there, hitting, blood
all over them, the big eyes of the rabbits
shining out of the dust, their screams cutting
the air, boys shouting & the older men sat
back, watching, smoked their brownpaper Durhams
& smiled, thinking of the rich feed to come.

MURIEL RUKEYSER: *Cannibal Bratuscha*

Have you heard about Mr. Bratuscha?
He led an orderly life
With a splendid twelve-year-old daughter,
A young and passionate wife—
    Bratuscha, the one they call Cannibal.

Spring evening on Wednesday,
The sky is years ago;
The girl has been missing since Monday,
Why don't the birches blow?
    And where's their daughter?

Nine miles to the next village
Deep in the forested past—
Wheatland, marshland, daisies
And a gold slender ghost.
    It's very difficult to keep them safe.

She hasn't been seen and it's Thursday.
Down by the river, raped?
Under the birches, murdered?
Don't let the fiend escape.
    First, we'll track him down and catch him.

The river glittering in sunlight,
The woods almost black—and she
Was always a darling, the blonde young daughter,
Gone gone vanished away.
    They say Bratuscha is ready to talk.

O God he has told the whole story;
Everything; he has said
That he killed his golden daughter
He ate her, he said it!
    Eaten by the cannibal, Cannibal Bratuscha.

Down at the church her mother
In the confession booth—

She has supported his story,
She has told the priest the truth;
      Horror, and now the villagers gather.

They are ready to lynch Bratuscha,
Pounding at his door—
Over the outcries of the good people
Hear the cannibal roar—
      He will hold out, bar the doorway, fight to the death.

But who is this coming, whose shadow
Runs down the river road?
She is coming, she is running, she is
Alive and abroad—
      She is here, she is well, she was in the next village.

The roaring dreams of her father:
He believed all he confessed—
And the mother was threatened with hellfire
By the village priest
      If she didn't tell everything, back up what Bratuscha said.

This all took place some time ago
Before all villages joined—
When there were separate, uncivilized people,
Only the birds, only the river, only dreams and the wind.
      She had just gone off for a few days, with a friend.

But O God the little Bratuscha girl
What will become of her?
Her mother is guilt suggestion panic
Her father of dreams, a murderer
      And in waking and in fantasy and now and forever.

Who will help her and you and me and all those
Children of the assumption of guilt

And the roaring fantasy of nightmare
The bomb the loathing all dreams split
  Upon this moment and the future and all unborn children.

We must go deep go deep in our lives and our dreams—
Remember Cannibal Bratuscha his wife and his young child
And preserve our own ideas of guilt
Of innocence and of the blessed wild
  To live out our own lives to make our own freedom to make
   the world.

PHILIP WHALEN: *To Edward Dahlberg*

the last secret batty American genius,
 bright gargoyle bellybutton living disciple of Thomas Nashe,

Let's you and me go burn down a couple universities—
 Fairy International, flap your mothy wings to speed the blaze

   !   !   !
    O HECATOMB OF IGNORANCE

LARRY EIGNER: *De Edw. Dahlberg*

What isn't
borne, or
to
be borne, the

  school, life, maybe,

shrugged off, in a
  nutshell

   pretzel

    space
     may be
    the world

PHILIP O'CONNOR: *Poor lines to
rich integrity*

Even bad cheese fills a cavity
but bad writing makes it bigger;
a whore may deliver a body
but a hack unleashes a snigger

traveling like a wireworm through the lines
of our truth, our daily bread.
Of hucksters the very worst
are they who sell the heart to the head.

Mr. Dahlberg, I do not "know you"
better knowing, as I should instead,
a little, stormy book that D. H. L. introduced
who had taken his life to bed

and by her had many dreams
and many children still unwed:
and I knew you then as one of those
of whom "failure" can never be said;

for we only fail in the wrong attempt
of selling the heart to the head;
Mr. Dahlberg, you keep open a heart entire
and are true to the wife you have wed:

true enough (I hope)
to pardon the rusty machine of my rhyme—
in time, in time.

JACK KEROUAC: *To Edward Dahlberg*

Don't use the telephone.
People are never ready to answer it.
Use poetry.

148

GILBERT NEIMAN: *To E. D.*
(from another ex-cancerous Kansan)

What do your words say
They say this in Nineveh
Life now
Worse than Dante's

When you go to Tibet
After you kill yourself
They will tell you there
That you should not have stored

So many images loved and abhorred
By those who love and abhor you

You come out of a Stygian ecstasy

Peer
Seer

No more
Magic
Words
Now

But when you die

PHOTO BY RALPH EUGENE MEATYARD.

"BOTTOM DOGS", PHOTO BY SIMPSON KALISHER.

JAMES BROUGHTON: *Notes found in the margins of Dahlberg's books*

To have great poets must there be dreadful societies too?

*

Poets are defined by businessmen, as everything is defined by its opposite. And opposites are secretly in love with each other.

*

To be high-minded leads one's feet up a mountain. But the dust of the plain clings to one's shoes.

*

Even if a great philosopher can be refuted, said Valéry, his thought remains an astonishing work of art.

*

Opinions are in the end only opinions. What makes the difference is how they are expressed.

*

If a man has no style, he is not yet a man.

*

Pleasure quite possibly is a great good in its own right. But to expand the spirit we must shrink the flesh, said Buddha and Christ. At the same time: "Be primordial or decay."

*

The fool who persists in his folly becomes wise enough to know the difference.

*

Poetry may be a criticism of life, but life triumphs over all criticism. And what have we ultimately but "a warring peace, a sweet wound, an agreeable evil"?

WALTER LOWENFELS:
From "Paragraphs for Dahlberg"

Einstein was right: we all hear the same things. Only our ears are shaped differently.

*

With poems, one reader is a miracle; two, a mass movement.

*

Julius Tuvim told us: The more dangerous it gets to speak, the more painful it is to keep silent.

*

The artist might be described as one who masters the technique of saying the obvious without being executed first.

*

An artist like Whitman is a menace: you can't write like him; you can't write without him.

*

In North America there are two classes: the disgusting and the disgusted.

*

Man is the 24th of the placentals to enter the world with a death sentence.

*

One function of the critic is to distinguish neurasthenia from music.

*

This talk about the artist's humanity makes me wonder. All Leadbelly seems to have done is to share his vast 12-string lonesomeness.

*

So much fuss about the Truth! As if we didn't know it's a cluttered desk full of pencils, scraps of paper, paste, scissors, and the book you are stealing from.

DRAWING BY JAMES MCGARRELL. (THOSE PICTURED ARE STEIGLITZ,
STEPHEN CRANE, HARTE CRANE, SHERWOOD ANDERSON, MARSDEN HARTLEY,
THEODORE DREISER AND WILLIAM CARLOS WILLIAMS.)

JOEL OPPENHEIMER:
Birthday presence

despairing, he
fixed me with
the good eye, staring
at the world, as
usual, with the
other.
      if you
wouldn't drink in
bars, he said.
         if
you'd learn your
greek and latin.

i've read your
stuff, he said, and
you could be great.

if only, he said, you'd
follow rare ben
jonson.
      edward, said
i, ben got stoned in
the mermaid every
goddamned night.

ben jonson never drank,
said edward, and i almost
believed him.
       as he
almost believed himself.

and what a pair to
drink with, if the
world be fair to men.

and what a pair to write
with, if the world
be fair at all.

STANLEY BURNSHAW: *Seedling air*
(*for Edward Dahlberg*)

I do not change. I grow
The kernel that my hair,
My thought, my blood, enflames.
I sing my seedling air:

I shout this ancient air

Into the hail of days
That washes through my skin
To pound and drench my bones.
I keep my light within:

My light burns on within

Flooding my endless rooms
Of pure and feeling brain
Till streams of wisdom-warmth
Murmur within each vein:

They chant within each vein

Will to withstand unchanged
All grindings of that air
Though torrents press down hail
Harsher than they would bear:

For what has will to bear

But outward change that strives
To enter in, and breath
But inner bloom that wavers
Under the hail of death?

GUS BLAISDELL: *The American Caliban*

A part, yet still apart, I see you stand,
The thyrsus of intelligence in hand;
Your rage reveals this beast that prowls this land:

Slick with excremental slime, and tumid glands,
Caliban, laureled bloody with barbed wire,
A fallen brute, his itching flesh afire,
Grabs his swollen manhood; with callused hands,
With muscles corded, bunched, with heaving chest,
Excoriates the foreskin's palimpsest.

Such visions nauseate, yet state our plight.
So sing thy thewy line, chant out thy light,
Good angered heart beat passion out of night!

CHRISTOPHER MIDDLETON:
Inspirationless thought

Surprise surprise surprise
to find, behind
the red brick of a Vic-
torian turreted Southern Electric
railway station in S.E.23, in a
row of old Londinium
kitschglass detective fiction cookbooks
& manuals of salvation damp & bent
by ghoulfog soot worms mildew several bombs
hardbound the live body of his Matrix radix
for the price of a pint
From Flushing to Calvary

157

THOMAS MCGRATH: *The landscape inside me*

Here I go riding through my morning self.
Between West Elbow and Little East Elbow;
Between Hotspur Heart and the Islands of Langerhans,
On the Rock Island Line of my central nervous system.

And I note the landscape which inhabits me—
How excellent in the morning to be populated by trees!
And all the hydrants are manned by dogs
And every dog is a landscape full of fleas;

And every flea is an index to the mountains!
I am well pleased with myself that I've kept the mountains.
What I can't understand is why I've kept the smog,
But since it inhabits me, why should I deny it?

Especially, why deny it on a morning like this—
When I've a large unidentified star in my left
Elbow and in my head a windy palette of birds,
And a lively line-storm crossing my pancreas?

FREDERICK ECKMANN:
On this auspicious occasion

Lord, as old as this weary
wicked century,

but infinitely younger:
pure Greek

like Empedocles & Heraclitus
before the shits

took it
all over . . .

158

RONALD BAYES:
For Edward Dahlberg

Once a general
told me at breakfast
"All of my friends
are dead
or in jail
or in power."

Ain't many of us
can go those three/
thirds of the way!
But I thought I
understood, and
despite
his being a general
did him a garland,
automatically.

Bless the word,
as you would.
Bless the world.

& you should see
the one woven
in Tokyo for you,
this day.

ANTHONY KERRIGAN: *South of France/North of Spain,*
April/May, 1958

                                        Edward Dahlberg

spoke of the daughter of Lot
                    at Foix:
discovered the Hittite name of Pius IV
                    at Toulouse,
where he denied six Apostles church burial:
invented old generations in the night
                    at Bordeaux:
debated the death of St. Vincent
                    in Teresa's Avila:
denounced the Moabites outside
                    Unamuno's Salamanca:
warned against the sodomitic Figure of the
                    Right Hand at Dos Aguas'
palace in Valencia.

                                        Edward Dahlberg

with whom I'd as lief pray, or wail or sorrow
                    in these, or other, cathedral towns.

DRAWING BY J. KEARNS.

ANSELM HOLLO: *Fest haiku for Edward Dahlberg*

clear spring mountain river
rock-rasp voice—ears, be proud: you
heard it, come what may.

PHOTO BY HAGEMEYER. PRESENTED TO ROSA SHUSER BY DAHLBERG,
DATED JULY 27, 1932, CARMEL-BY-THE-SEA, CALIFORNIA.

1a. *Bottom Dogs.* With an introduction by D. H. Lawrence. London: G. P. Putnam's Sons [1929]. "This edition is limited to 520 copies for sale by private subscription only."

b. Trade edition.

c. New York: Simon and Schuster, 1930.

d. Pocket edition in wrappers, with a new preface by the author. [San Francisco]: City Lights Books [© 1961].

2. *Kentucky Blue Grass Henry Smith.* With drawings by Augustus Peck. Cleveland: The White Horse Press, 1932. An expanded version of Section 2, Part 6 of *From Flushing to Calvary.* "Limited to ninety-five numbered copies printed by hand on Georgian paper. Of this edition ten copies numbered one to ten have been signed by the author."

3a. *From Flushing to Calvary.* New York: Harcourt, Brace & Company, 1932.

b. London: G. P. Putnam's Sons [1933].

4. *Those Who Perish.* New York: The John Day Company [© 1934]. There are two states of binding: one black cloth, the other (probably a remainder binding) orange cloth.

5a. *Do These Bones Live.* New York: Harcourt, Brace & Company [© 1941].

b. A revised edition with a foreword by Herbert Read, published as *Sing O Barren.* London: George Routledge & Sons, 1947.

163

c. Another revision with a preface by Sir Herbert Read and forty-two drawings by James Kearns, published as *Can These Bones Live.* New York: New Directions [© 1960]. There are two states of binding: the first blue cloth, the second tan paper over boards.

d. Pocket edition. [Ann Arbor]: The University of Michigan Press [1967]. Ann Arbor Paperbacks AA128.

6*a. The Flea of Sodom.* With an introduction by Herbert Read. London: Peter Nevill Limited [1950].

b. American edition from imported sheets of London edition. New York: New Directions [1950]. Directions Series 18.

7*a. The Sorrows of Priapus.* With drawings by Ben Shahn. [Norfolk, Conn.: New Directions, 1957.] "This first edition of *The Sorrows of Priapus* is limited to one hundred and fifty copies on mould-made Arches paper. . . . Signed by the author and the artist." Inserted in each copy of the book is one of four different lithograph drawings by Shahn.

b. Trade edition is a reduced offset printing from the limited edition. There are two states of the dust jacket: one that advertises the limited edition on the back flap and one that does not.

8. *Moby Dick—An Hamitic Dream.* Teaneck, N.J.: Fairleigh Dickinson University [© 1960]. Caption title; offprint from *The Literary Review,* Vol. 4, No. 1. Includes portraits of Dahlberg and Herman Melville by James Kearns.

9*a. Truth Is More Sacred.* A critical exchange on modern literature by Edward Dahlberg and Herbert Read: James Joyce, D. H. Lawrence, Henry James, Robert Graves, T. S. Eliot, Ezra Pound. New York: Horizon Press [1961].

b. London: Routledge & Kegan Paul [1961].

10*a. Because I Was Flesh.* Autobiography. [Norfolk, Conn.]: New Directions [1964]. Advance copy issued in wrappers for promotional purposes.

b. Trade edition. There are two states of the dust jacket, each with a different list of readers' statements on the back.

c. Second printing.

d. Pocket edition in wrappers. [New York]: New Directions [1967]. New Directions Paperback 227.

e. Italian translation. *Mia madre Lizzie*. Traduzione di Rodolfo Nil-cock. [Torino]: Einaudi [© 1966].

f. German translation. *Denn ich war Fleisch*. [München]: R. Piper [1968].

11*a*. *Alms for Oblivion*. Essays, with a foreword by Sir Herbert Read. Minneapolis: University of Minnesota Press [© 1964].

b. First issue consisted of a handful of copies with suppressed text on page 53.

c. Second issue with canceled leaf 53/54.

d. Second printing.

e. Pocket edition in wrappers. Minneapolis: University of Minnesota Press [1967]. Minnesota Paperbacks MP5.

12. *Reasons of the Heart*. [New York]: Horizon Press [© 1965].

13. *Cipango's Hinder Door*. Austin: The University of Texas [© 1965]. Tower Series No. 6. Published March 1966.

14. *Epitaphs of Our Times*. Letters. New York: George Braziller [1967]. Copies placed on sale in December 1966.

15*a*. *The Edward Dahlberg Reader*. Edited and with an introduction by Paul Carroll. [New York]: New Directions [© 1967].

b. Pocket edition in wrappers. [New York]: New Directions [© 1967]. New Directions Paperback NDP246.

16*a*. *The Leafless American*. Edited and with an introduction by Harold Billings. [Sausalito, California]: Roger Beacham, Publisher [© 1967]. First issue consisted of about two dozen copies, with misplaced lines on pages 4 and 97.

b. Second issue, with leaves 3/4 and 97/98 canceled, and a period inserted in holograph at line 18 on page 27.

17. *The Carnal Myth*. New York: Weybright and Talley [c. 1968].

18. *The Leafless American*. Broadside poem. Fifty copies printed for friends of Bernice and Harold Billings. Austin: Christmas 1968.

19. *Confessions*. Literary autobiography. To be published by George Braziller in 1970.

20. Untitled volume of literary portraits. To be published by Weybright and Talley when completed.

1900	Edward Dalberg (spelling later changed) born July 22, 1900, in a charity hospital in Boston, the son of Elizabeth Dalberg and Saul Gottdank.
1901–5	Travels with his mother to London, Dallas, Memphis, New Orleans, Louisville, and Denver.
1905–6	Lizzie settles with her son in Kansas City, where she operates the Star Lady Barbershop at 16 East Eighth Street.
1907–8	Edward in Catholic orphanage in Kansas City.
1912–17	Edward an inmate of the Jewish Orphan Asylum in Cleveland.
1917–21	Works as messenger boy for Western Union in Cleveland and in Kansas City stockyards; hoboes through the West; is private in U.S. Army; lives in Los Angeles.
1922–23	Attends University of California, Berkeley.
1922	Dahlberg's first published work, an essay titled "The Sick, the Pessimist, and the Philosopher," appears in *The Occident,* November 1922.
1924–25	Attends Columbia University and takes B.S. in philosophy.
1926	Teaches at James Madison High School, New York.

1926–28 Lives in Paris, Monte Carlo, Brussels. Writes *Bottom Dogs* after several novels are discarded. Changes spelling of name.

1929 First part of *Bottom Dogs* published as "Beginnings and Continuations of Lorry Gilchrist" in *This Quarter*, No. 4. (Issue also includes two poems, a short story, and an essay.) *Bottom Dogs* published by Putnam's in London.

1930 *Bottom Dogs* published by Simon and Schuster in New York.

1931 Contributes to *Poetry* and *Pagany*.

1932 *From Flushing to Calvary* published by Harcourt, Brace. *Kentucky Blue Grass Henry Smith* (an expanded version of Section 2 of Part 6 of preceding title) published in an edition of 95 copies by White Horse Press, Cleveland. Contributes to *The Nation* and *The New Republic*.

1933 *From Flushing to Calvary* published by Putnam's, London. Visits Berlin at time of Reichstag Fire and is beaten in the streets as a Jew.

1934 Anti-Nazi novel *Those Who Perish* published by John Day.

1935 Helps organize the first American Writers' Congress and presents paper, "Fascism and Writers."

1936 Portion of uncompleted novel, "Bitch Goddess," published in *Signature* magazine.

1937–40 Dahlberg variously in New York, Mexico City, San Antonio, Kansas City, Chicago, Boston, Washington, New Orleans, Los Angeles. Works on *Do These Bones Live*.

1941 *Do These Bones Live* published by Harcourt, Brace.

1942 Marries Winifred Sheehan Moore, mother of his sons Geoffrey and Joel.

1947 *Sing O Barren* (a revision of *Do These Bones Live*) published by Routledge, London.

1950 *The Flea of Sodom* published by Peter Nevill, London; sheets imported by New Directions for American edition. Marries R'lene LaFleur Howell.

1950–53   Lives in New York and in Berkeley, Topanga, and Santa Monica, California. Contributes regularly to *Tomorrow* and *The Freeman*.

1953–56   Lives in Santa Monica and Berkeley.

1956–57   Travels to Bornholm, Malaga, Ascona, Paris, Mallorca.

1957   *The Sorrows of Priapus* published by New Directions.

1958–64   Lives in Mallorca, New York, and Dublin.

1960   *Can These Bones Live* revised and reissued. Dahlberg receives award from Longview Foundation for a section of *Because I Was Flesh,* published in *Big Table*.

1961   *Truth Is More Sacred* (with Sir Herbert Read) published by Routledge & Paul, London, and Horizon Press. Dahlberg receives grant from National Institute of Arts and Letters.

1964   *Because I Was Flesh* published by New Directions. *Alms for Oblivion* published by University of Minnesota Press.

1965   Dahlberg returns to Kansas City from Mallorca as Professor of English Literature at University of Missouri. *Reasons of the Heart* published by Horizon Press. Dahlberg receives grant from Rockefeller Foundation.

1966   *Cipango's Hinder Door* published by University of Texas.

1967   *Epitaphs of Our Times* published by Braziller; *The Edward Dahlberg Reader* by New Directions; and *The Leafless American* by Roger Beacham. Marries Julia Lawlor.

1968   *The Carnal Myth* published by Weybright and Talley. Elected to National Institute of Arts and Letters.

1968–69   Lives in New York, Dublin, Barcelona, and Geneva. Returns to New York to complete the tales for *The Tailor's Daughter* (Roger Beacham) and his literary autobiography, *Confessions* (Braziller). Begins a volume of literary portraits for Weybright and Talley.

EDWARD DAHLBERG: *Some books every intelligent reader and writer should take unto his heart and into his head*

Shestov, *In Job's Balances*.
Shestov, *Penultimate Words*.
Rozanov, *Solitario*.
Grote, *History of Greece*.
Amiel, *Journal*.
Diogenes Laertius, *Lives of the Greek Philosophers*.
A. B. Cook, *Zeus*.
Sallust, *Catiline*.
La Bruyère, *Characters*.
I. D. D'Israeli, *Curiosities of Literature*.
I. D. D'Israeli, *Miscellanies*.
Charles Lamb, *Letters*.
Coleridge, *Letters*.
Ruskin, *Unto This Last*.
Postgate, *Out of the Past*.
Kropotkin, *Mutual Aid*.
Rosa Luxemburg, *Letters*.
Pausanias, *Description of Greece*.
Quevedo, *Visions*.
Theodor Gomperz, *Greek Thinkers*.
Lucian (tr. Jasper Mayne).
Burnet, *Early Greek Philosophy*.
Diodorus of Siculus.
Strabo, *Geography*.

169

Maxim Gorki, *Remembrances of Leo Tolstoi.*
Merezhkowski, *Tolstoi: Man and Artist.*
Book of Psalms (tr. Christopher Smart).
Morris Jastrow, *The Book of Job.*
Plautus, *The Comedies.*
Epigrams from the Greek Anthology (tr. Mackail).
William Hazlitt, *Liber Amoris.*
Franz Oppenheimer, *The State.*
J. A. Stewart, *The Myths of Plato.*
Erasmus, *Familiar Colloquies.*
P. F. Brissenden, *IWW.*
Sylvanus G. Morley, *The Ancient Maya.*
Morris Jastrow, *The Gentle Cynic.*
Morris Jastrow, *The Song of Songs.*
Livy (tr. Philemon Holland).
Plutarch, *Moralia.*
Wallis Budge, *The Book of Treasuries.*
Wallis Budge, *The Mummy.*
Josephus, *Jewish Antiquities and the Jewish Wars* (tr. Whiston).
Charles Baudelaire, *The Intimate Journals* (tr. Christopher Isherwood).
Thomas Traherne, *Centuries.*
Alexander Gilchrist, *The Life of William Blake.*
Montaigne (tr. Florio).
Buffon, *Natural History* (1603 edition).
Gustave Flaubert, *Letters.*
Pío Baroja, *Egolatry.*
Miguel de Unamuno, *The Soliloquies and Conversations of Don Quixote.*
Garcilaso de la Vega, *Royal Commentaries of the Incas.*
Dionysius of Halicarnassus, *Roman Antiquities.*
Sir Thomas Browne, *Enquiries into Vulgar and Common Errors*
Sir Thomas Browne, *The Garden of Cyrus.*
Hazlitt, *Lectures on the English Comic Writers.*
Winterslow, *Essays.*

PORTRAIT BUST OF DAHLBERG BY AUBREY SCHWARTZ.
PHOTO BY BOB CATO.

EDWARD DAHLBERG: *Confessions*

> *But Age, allas! that al wole envenyme,*
> *Hath me biraft my beautee and my pith.*
> —Chaucer

So much of me has departed. Long ago I left massy tufts of my hair in boxcars, and in cheap, venereal hotel rooms in the Mexican quarter of Los Angeles, and all for a pence of a thought. How hard and usurious is the Muse, exacting the cruelest payment for the mite she gives.

My youth is clean gone, and for a cock of prose thin and dwarfed as the lichen in the Barren Grounds. I sigh for vision, and know not what shirt I wore that day. I examine my hands and wonder whose they are; my nose is a stranger to my face. When I think I know, I do not know. If I am quiet, impatience were better; if choleric, it is a dudgeon day. That's how it is with me.

I've got no theories to peddle, for I hawk parables, or chew my mouldy weather, and that's good too. That's how it is with me.

I swallow people's scoffs, and that's not a dirty meal either; in the long run, I like that I've got to bolt down. That's how it is with me.

When I don't tremble, I am full of multitude. Would you be

This extract includes the 28th and 40th (and final) sections of Edward Dahlberg's *Confessions,* to be published by George Braziller, Inc., late in 1970.—*Ed.*

prophetic or sink into the dotage of the Many? Touch me, and you'll be soothsayers. You don't think so, I do. That's how it is with me.

O hungry ones, I am starved, and I drink the rains and the heavens. When I'm empty, and there are freezing steppes in my spirit, I disgorge my Muse, the Void. What a constellation is Nothing. Still what have I gotten out of it? But everything matters. That's how it is with me.

Wherever I am I wish to be elsewhere. I leave my unfriended steps in last year's snow, and give my confidence to a sharper in today's rain. That's how it is with me.

I try to mend my lot, though I am my portion. I endeavor to pick myself up when I fall, but it is better there. Truth has given me nothing, yet that nothing I require. That's how it is with me.

As I write this I'm seated at a kitchen table in Geneva, in a pinched bald room of an old manor house where Voltaire once lived and wrote. My bones shake, and my pulses scarce murmur, yet I hope, poor fool that I am, to get off a line that flames like tow. And after that, what? I wait for the morrow, another guillotine morning. That's how it is with me.

But it is better to gnaw my secondhand sour sighs, and eat old groans, and suck up the foul drizzle of hackneyed disappointments —better to be pinheaded François Villon, with his long-knived nose, and chew my days that are bread "black as a maulkin" than to nuzzle at the slops of other people's opinions. The real sacrilege is the low farce, everyday life. That's how it is with me.

Jesus was a nervous man and just as unsure of himself as I am, and though nothing can be proved I have all the evidence in my vest pocket. Who understands the divine man who begged the world to smite him on the other cheek? Long ago I found out that only he who requires love most of all is absolutely crestfallen when nobody even bothers to do him the slightest mischief.

The poor holy ghost appeared before the disciples, and although he had been absent for the shortest while, they didn't know him. They had eaten together day after day, gone on foot to Capernaum, walked about the Sea of Galilee together and discussed various stiff-necked infidel towns yet the twelve looked at him without a tithe of recognition. He had to tell them to handle him and *see*. Be plain, is there any other way of seeing except by touching? I am that sort of specter and, though profane, a distant kin of his; for every friend I ever had has been a blundering stranger who did not know me. How many times they cogged me, or stabbed me with a simper; just a passing leer grieves my entrails. Still, if I were sharp as they it would be bad for me. That's how it is with me.

When someone strokes my shoulder or caresses my coat lapel, I'm lost. Once a rogue grinned at me, and though I don't care for a smile that is no more than cosmetics on the mouth, could I turn my back on him and step on his feelings? I admit it: Christ is my sort of poet. Once you decline to turn the other cheek you're ignominious. So while I bent my neck toward him he picked my purse. Suppose I had ignored him, I would have been spiteful, and malice is lust. Of course my wallet sorrowed for many weeks and even now it hasn't gotten over that wicked experience. But if I hadn't been deceived could I possess what belongs to me?

Then a former convict came to my apartment. I knew he was a confidence man, and he realized right away I could be taken. But didn't he know me? And is that evil? When he asked me for twenty-five dollars could I refuse him? He said he had a ring at the pawnbroker's which he would redeem and would return the money the next day. I knew he would not come back. That was his greatest unkindness, for we could have talked some more and exchanged the cruelties in our lives. I never saw him again. Yet why should he imagine I would not receive or embrace him? I always forgive my enemies; they're so close to me. That's how it is with me.

How hard it is to know what to do with one's self. The shoe knows it must be worn; otherwise it's been abandoned. A button understands that it hangs by a thread to a coat. A rock knows what to do in the fog or a long mean rain. A headland is just as calm in foul weather as it is in a mild sun. The shingle at Tierra del Fuego doesn't show any disgust with carrion whale washed up on it. A pebble knows how to handle a pack of wolvish winds that beat it all day long. But I'm thrown down by a trifling slight. I offer affection to people who mean nothing to me, and am courteous to one who has done his best to hinder me; shrewd as he is he doesn't know that's my lot and he's served me. A passerby roughly jostles me, and though I beg his pardon for doing it his silence cuts me. That's how it is with me.

What bothers me more than anything else is a day of zero. When nothing happens I cry out for an event, an unlooked-for pain, a stitch in my side, or I moan for long-standing scums of water; I boil over everything. Aristotle says worms are born in snow. Would that I were a frosty maggot, but that would be bad for my nature. That's how it is with me.

Suppose Christ had not drunk his cup of affliction, or that the cruel Roman Titus had not slaughtered a million Jews in ancient Jerusalem, what could I now do with a so-called life that had not made everyone suffer? That's how it is with me.

> The whole of this material universe of
> ours, with all its suns and its milky
> ways—is nothing.—Tolstoy.

I had fled from the universal theology of lucre but could not avoid the snare of politics. I had reached the end, which is another path to perception. My skies were sackcloth, my distempered lakes were dried up, my body a dead gully. The abyss is no-feeling, that is the ultimate despondency. When I'm cauterized, flea'd or bled, I want to feel it.

The first intimation of my condition came not from my intellect but from my foot. Ill luck had been settling in my joints and unsinging knees; worst of all, my feet were forceless sinking shadows. When the feet despair the mind is a Tartarus of black humors. The neck, the arms, the elbows, and especially the feet know what is going on long before the head has intelligence of it. One thing I want to make plain is that the mind is the most ignorant part of the body. Could I only forget my old footsteps I might cure a jot of my nature.

175

Realizing I could cony-catch myself better than any enemy, I came to another indecision. I resolved to make the journey alone, with nothing to guide me except the oar of the prophet Tiresias, also blind, which Odysseus had gotten. I saw it was either the Many or the Socratic hemlock of ostracism—a ticklish choice, but life took care of that.

I dimly understood I would never be out of the forest, so deep and wild was the dusky foliage of Nodh in my breast. As a writer I had not even begun my apprenticeship. It took more than the strength of the phoenix for me to raise my maimed pinions from the ashes of my brute scrawl.

Wherever I went I was the victim of a doltish Communist Ajax ready to slay me with his dullness. Everything got worse though nothing was ever any good. Unable to escape my persecutors I brooded over the disappearing American earth; as Péguy said, the world had become a people-less land. The machine had displaced human beings.

What was my Atlean heresy? Gibbeted because I had a great dislike for the coarse gallows scribblings of Hemingway and Caldwell, I was the meal and booty of the rapacious salt tooth of Rumor. The Stalinist myrmidons spread the report I was an informer. Would to heaven I could spy upon my own feelings. I could not eschew their fangs of malice: "Thy reason, dear venom, give thy reason," laments Shakespeare, and Ben Jonson asserts: "I am beholden to calumny."

The Stalinist book slayers were stationed on almost every paper and magazine that claimed importance. What wolves were the Communist lambs who spoiled the vines of any writer who abhorred the banner of homogeneity. They pretended my volumes did not exist, and cast them into Tophet without a reviewer's obituary notice. "As good almost kill a man as kill a good book," it is written in Milton's *Areopagitica*. Whether I was in New York, Los Angeles, or San Francisco, I was pursued by the beagles, the Stalinists and FBI agents.

Man covers the planet with gore for justice, but where is it? Tamburlaine spilled far less blood than Stalin. Can anybody imagine that Breznev, the czarist clerk garbed in the drab vestments and chasuble, the double-breasted suit of the assassin businessman, who impudently intones "Holy Russia" and "Our Mother Land," is a Lycurgus or an Agesilaus? Little wonder that Leopardi saw the world as a vast league of criminals ruthlessly warring against a few virtuous madmen. The soul pants for the tender frolicking hills, the small meditative brooks, the miracle of human warmth, and an apocryphal Eden. In the Jewish legends it is said that dying Adam asked Seth his son to fetch oil from the Tree of Knowledge, but Paradise had vanished.

I fell into hourless Orcus, and the leaden fog on the rigging of my soul was frozen hard. I saw that the Barren Grounds is not the coldest region on the earth: it is the human heart. I stuffed my ribs and naked moaned: "My name, my name, thou hast been besmirched, every rogue has bayed thee. Be quiet, poor flensed waif, and sit in the dusty dry corner of thy self." I shrouded myself in seven syllables of silence, in seven leaves of years, within seven Ephesian graves.

Would I ever find a northwest passage to the Moluccas? That could not be. I've always been a helpless ninny, an inexplicable ludicrous one. Imagine I sought affection from people I never needed; they were senseless and droll enough to suppose I required them. That was the only hoax I was ever able to impose upon these average unfeeling noddles. Naturally I gather together a few persons now and then to decoy me. A man has to provide himself with a covey of Judases; that's what is called life.

Then I wrote books, a useless occupation, and I would have done something else had I thought of it. Seneca advises his readers that a man must do something though it be to no purpose. Besides, I got into a squabble with myself about truth and justice. Am I really serious about this? How should I know? All I can say is though I am no astute worldly Pontius Pilate I ask what is truth since no one lives by it. " 'And there is some good in the world,' replied Candide. 'Maybe so,' said Martin, 'but it has escaped my knowledge.' "

No matter how often I studied Homer I could not be sane about the vain and imbecile pursuit of wisdom. The Sirens endeavor to tempt Odysseus to approach the perfidious rocks by offering him what no mortal can attain, knowledge.

Then I fell into another predicament: what mite of consciousness could ever be mine? The more I am on guard against my emptiness and fatuity the more obtuse I am. How can one be vigilant twenty-four hours of the day? Not even the disciples could remain awake long enough for the vigil. I am sure they were automatic. Did they walk to Capernaum? I doubt it; they thought they did. They never lived; nobody has. No, I am not quibbling: I do not believe I exist. Suppose I'm wrong, it won't be momentous anyway. The universe is a slumbering animal that has visions. "I think the world's asleep," says Lear.

Descartes was sure of his paltry dictum: "I think, therefore I am." But I think and am not. I grant either way there is no evidence. Our short pilgrimage is obviously one of renunciations. At first we trust what we are sure we see, but this is a seminal delusion. Then little by little, as our rude and coarse physical forces dwindle, we become extremely suspicious, and begin to assume the earth's a ruse and that we have been taken in all the while. What are these things since everyone perceives them differently? I came to feel that space is a void and time the flux and ebb of a dying dream.

When people die we very soon forget how they looked. Did they ever exist is our unrelieved groan. It never occurred to me that I would regard trees, the ground, a shingle, the sea as God's baubles. Heraclitus states: "All things we see when awake are death." One can go on and on.

Meanwhile I have accumulated a pile of wrinkles which are basely attributed to time by toad-spotted heads. Once in a while I regard a new crease around my mouth as a frightful defeat and my downfall. I have another fear which contradicts whatever I have said. Although I have confessed I don't care a tittle for my intelligence, what will happen if my faculties begin to flag? Lucretius revealed that "when Democritus was warned by his ripe old age that the memory-bringing motions of his mind were languishing, he spontaneously offered his head to death."

What has the Worm taught me? I believe that Shakespeare's hundred and fifty-four sonnets were a hundred and fifty-four Gethsemane nights. Is that all? Is there nothing else? I pity the squalid drabs of the bribed Muses and pickthank feelings who've never been ripened by shame, mire, the ditch of humiliation. Not one author has sung the song of the dying swan, what Socrates referred to as the thinker's last senilia. They linger on, their wings shriveled, dissipated echoes of their youthful dotages. "Many a one, alas, waxeth too old for his truths," said Nietzsche. Would that I weren't a writer; since I am, I'd like to produce one page that is a replica of the handkerchief of St. Veronica upon which was impressed the divine and tragic features of Jesus.

I have another pelting vexation. Suppose there is a Creator, or a Demiurge who framed day and night, will it make any difference? Won't I arise in the morning petulant because there is rime on the windowsill, a cramp in the small part of my back, acid mildew in my lungs, or my head is clogged with fenny yesterdays? And if there is no God, will it not be the same? I'll die anyway.

Would I had a dram of calm. Will the grave provide it? Is death total cessation, or may it not be a wailing and gnashing of the grieving bones? There might be a grain of truth in this, for the body is no liar. Let me taste the constellations when I go my way unhindered to the great Worm, enjoy one infinite second of quiet.

Since there's no solution I stalk the stage in buskins though I speak in my comic socks, and I dismiss the immense self-delusion, life, and bid farewell to the world with: "Sir, money is a whore."

This is not all. Another small matter frets me: why am I obscure to myself? Could I understand my experience, I would annihilate myself. However, as nature will do it for me, I sha'n't bother. It just occurred to me: Is God acquainted with Himself? All He can utter is: I am that I am. Is that a great revelation? Shakespeare, a better poet than God, is as vague; he merely mimicks the Lord and says: I am that I am.

That cutpurse I venerate, François Villon, palmed off this mournful stave: "I know the doublet by its collar; I know the monk by his habit; I know the master by his servant; I know the nun by her veil; I know the sharper by his jargon; I know fools fed on creams; I know wine by its barrel; I know all, except myself."

What else? I'm as lost as I was. Nobody has ever found himself. What I am searching for is a man with an unbearable void within him. I am seeking myself.

I confess I do not know my own bounds. Be done, ye caitiff cowards who announce your limits. I need stellar aetiologies.

No secular person, I am the small gleanings of many devout sages. This book has been hanging over my head like the rock of Tantalus. I have battered mountains, torn up seas as elephants in rage break grass by the roots, for a metaphor.

This is a song of no-knowledge, a chant of shame. What else can a memoir be but an enchiridion of chagrins? If I have not divulged all, it is that life is illicit. St. Paul saw in a vision things "unlawful to utter." I walk upon my hurts which readers entitle my books. Sunset writes for me, and rain scribbles my woes. Forgive me, dear unknown readers, for I cannot pardon myself nor life.

Before it's all over with me I am going out into the world to swear at the most depraved and cunning of all harlots, Reason. Ye who demand evidence are the culprits, for I am the proof. When I am clean out of reason I am out of guile. Have you not learned that a logician will cut your heart into a thousand gammons and languorously champ it? Does this make me a weeping trunk of dust? Only a rationalist would so affront me.

In one respect I am resigned to be the staunch companion of Alone. A writer is a banished man. Euripides died in Macedonia; Thucydides wrote his history of the war between the Athenians and the Peloponnesians near the forest Scapte; Herodotus migrated to Thurii. While the "fishes are quivering on the horizon, and all the Wain lies over Taurus," I sacrifice reverently to the shade of holy outcast Spinoza.

In bringing this trembling exile book to a close, I pray it is the clay that smells of the flesh from which Prometheus moulded man. My own darkness, my wilderness, and the black Cain leaves crying in my breast are Odysseus' apostrophe to his own nature: "Endure, my soul, endure."

New York, Dublin, Barcelona, Tel Aviv, Geneva, New York, 1966–1970

Who are all these people, Herr Malthus?

Many of those printed in these pages, who have had their hands warmed and/or burned by the work and person of Edward Dahlberg, failed to send me contributors' notes or any sort of curriculum vitae. In some cases I must simply confess grave ignorance; in others my information is two years out of date. And since I am putting down said information on a Dutch freighter in mid-Atlantic, there is no access to library or telephone. My apologies, where due. Meantime, let us be leisurely and even a bit stylish in putting down what came to light during the years of producing this Festschrift. Say, for instance, I've put on plus-fours and want to characterize about 80 unknown persons to the likes of John Ruskin.   J. W.

BERENICE ABBOTT photographed Edward Dahlberg about 1940. For the life of me I cannot remember where I got the print—not from Miss Abbott. But I hope she does not object to its inclusion. She has had an important career in photography and her pioneer work in behalf of the work of Eugene Atget is especially notable. **RONALD BAYES** is a poet-in-residence at St. Andrews College, Laurinburg, North Carolina. Bayes's *The Book of the Turtle* (Olivant Press) has just been published. **HAROLD BILLINGS** is a slow-talking, sharp-eyed Texan from Fredericksburg out west of the LBJ country ("the best barbecue in Texas comes from a chicken-wire shack on North Llano Street—a moustached German named Burrer cooks it"), who knows more about the literary life of Edward Dahlberg than anybody else. Who else has ever turned up a pamphlet titled *Night-Gown Riders of America,* about the Silver Shirts, reprinted from *New Masses?* Mr. Billings' other bibliographical trove is the work of M. P. Shiel. He lives in Austin, Texas, and is in the Acquisitions Department of the University of Texas Library. He has been the most constant encouragement to the editing of this *Festschrift: "Git thar firsus with the thyrsus!"* **GUS BLAISDELL** is a walking disaster area in the Upper Rio Grande Valley, whose IQ is so high it has ruined most of the alleged minds in New Mexico, including his own. He used to do a lot of work for Alan Swallow in Denver; more recently he was with the University of New Mexico Press. God knows what he is doing now. Yvor Winters and J. V. Cunningham and Evan Connell have a strong and salty advocate, wherever Gus is. **KAY BOYLE** is a member of the English faculty at San Francisco State College. She is the author of more than twenty-five books, one of the most recent being a collection of short stories, *Nothing Ever Breaks Except the Heart* (Doubleday). Also recent are her editions of the memoirs of Robert McAlmon and Emanuel Carnevali. Miss Boyle's contribution to the *Festschrift* first appeared in *The Nation* (copyright 1967 by Kay Boyle) and is used with the permission of her agents. **COBURN BRITTON** is a partner, with Ben Raeburn, of Horizon Press in New York City, and is starting a new magazine, *Prose.* **JAMES BROUGHTON**—poet, playwright, film-maker—lives in Mill Valley, California. He teaches at San Francisco State College and is poetry critic for the *San Francisco Chronicle.* His books of poems include *True & False Unicorn, Musical Chairs,* and *Tidings.* In 1970, Jargon Society is publishing *The Long Undressing* (Collected Poems, 1949–69). His films include *The Pleasure Garden* and *The Bed.* **ANTHONY BURGESS'** article appeared in a somewhat different form in "Book World" and is reprinted with permission. I have not read his spate of novels; I haven't even read much of the recent collection of essays, *Urgent Copy;* but my intentions are honorable. Any writer who looks after mavericks like Dahlberg and Charles Doughty and Hubert Selby and Mervyn Peake is for me. And I want a chance to argue with his last postcard: "To hell with Bruckner, and not to hell with Ives or Delius. Or Satie. Or." **STANLEY BURNSHAW** is a poet, and an editor at Holt, Rinehart & Winston. Two of his books are *The Poem Itself* and *The Modern Hebrew Poem Itself.* His contribution to the *Festschrift* comes from his volume of poems, *Caged in an Animal's*

Mind (1963), and he writes this addendum: "My contribution must be the lyrical poem that I dedicated to Edward because it was the direct —unbelievably direct—outcome of a long, battling discussion we had had one night about six or seven years ago. We had been disagreeing on the matter of 'change'—how people do or do not change; and when we stopped talking and went our separate ways that midnight, I found myself unable to drop off to sleep. I kept up the argument, as it were, and some time around sunrise I got up, and in a half-sleep wrote down the words of the poem that you will find enclosed for your use. I don't think I had to make any changes from what had come onto the paper, for I was too half-asleep to have allowed my brain to interfere with the involuntary phrases. Anyway, the poem is as it was written, and it has remained the 'property' of Edward Dahlberg. . . ." **PAUL CARROLL** embodies most of the poetic flair to be found in "The-Place-of-the-Wild-Leeks" on the shores of Lake Michigan. Or "The-Swamp-of-the-Wild-Garlic." (*Chicago* means something like that in Welsh, etc.) Mr. Carroll has been for several years editing a series of "Big Table Books" for Follett Publishing Company. Observing Paul in action at the Red Star Inn and other haunts makes me want to see him play the lead in *The Baron Corvo Story.* **JULES CHAMETZKY** teaches at the University of Massachusetts and is editor of the *Massachusetts Review.* He publishes articles and reviews widely—on American realism, on the Thirties, and on American-Jewish writers. Mr. Chametzky's contribution appeared in slightly altered form in *Proletarian Literature of the Thirties* (Southern Illinois University Press, 1968), whom the author and I wish to thank for permission to reprint. **SID CHAPLIN** is a novelist and journalist whose work centers on the industrial and mining regions of the north of England. He lives in Newcastle-upon-Tyne, Northumberland. "I was up at Aydon Castle, not far from where you stayed, the day before I went into hospital. A ravine dropping sheer from the battlements, from which they 'hoyed' captured reivers. A little wood full of Iceland poppies like lemon butterflies . . ." **CID CORMAN** long ago fled the environs of Boston for the suburbs of Kyoto. His *Origin,* through its three series and its occasional books, has been uniquely important since it began in 1951. Corman is traveling in the United States this year on a lecture and reading tour. The constant, devotional, quiet life of letters has few better champions. **EDWARD DAHLBERG** has been "living" in New

York City; or, as he puts it: "work, more toil. Sitting at the table and the reading of many books may be a great weariness to Solomon, but it is the pith of my life. Let me say the *life* that matters; the everyday existence is not only unimportant, I do not know what it is." I should describe the provenance of the Dahlberg material in the *Festschrift*. The reading list is one of many that Dahlberg might quickly prepare for students and friends. Such a list as the present one reminds us that Mallarmé was dead wrong when he said: "La chair est triste, hélas, et j'ai lu tous les livres." *Nobody* has read all these books, perhaps including even E. D. I hope it will not affront some that Ronald Johnson saw fit to make a selection of passages from letters that Edward Dahlberg wrote to me over a period of years. I would have been more interested, for prime example, in the letters of Dahlberg to the young Charles Olson. They well may no longer exist—I am in no position to ask. As Mae West tells us: "The first thing to learn is to use what's lyin' around the house." Many persons have had useful protean correspondences with Dahlberg (viz., *Epitaphs of Our Times*). It happens that Mr. Johnson was privy to the receipt of most of these letters and to the answers they evoked. This is explanation enough. **GUY DAVENPORT** bides his time in Blue-Grass Limbo, living among his 10,000 books, going nowhere, owning no motorcar. This has made for a prodigious cultivation, the like of which is not seen in more than a handful per generation. Professor Davenport tries to teach Calvin, Homer, Louis Agassiz, Ezra Pound, Louis Zukofsky, and Stan Brakhage to towheaded disciples who go to the university bookstore and ask: "Do you have a poem-book on e.e. cummings?" He does reviews for *Life,* the *New York Times,* the *National Review;* he draws elegantly for *Arion* and for books by Hugh Kenner. He translates Archilochos and Sappho, Heraclitus and Alcman. He writes book-length poems like *Flowers & Leaves* (Jargon Society) in which Ives and Pound mix with the ghosts of Poloziano and Old Man Blake. He's a *sight,* as they say in his native South Carolina, and one of the reasons that the literary life in the United States is of occasional pleasure. **NICHOLAS DEAN** lives in Newcastle, Maine, with wife and five children, by an inlet full of excellent clams. He teaches in Portland at the art museum and likes to prowl the Kennebec and Androscoggin river valleys in search of the worlds of Hartley and E. A. Robinson. He made the photographs for my *Blues & Roots/Rue & Bluets,* out this year from Aperture/Grossman. He is working with Paul Metcalf on a book about the Potomac

184

Valley. **AUGUST DERLETH** is much too modest when he says he is just a large frog in a small pond. He has made his home, "Place of Hawks" in Sauk City, Wisconsin, into a one-man literary factory, and himself into one of our few real men of letters, writing 10,000 words a day every day of his life—reviewing, editing, and publishing Arkham House, responsible for the fame of H. P. Lovecraft, and our best press for fantasy and the supernatural tradition. By now he must have published 150 books of his own. Derleth is one of the only American writers I've ever met who felt "at home." If we had one or two such men in every state, we might have the ground for a literature other than that seen on the Johnny Carson show, in the slick magazines, and in "adult bookshops." He has a daughter, April, and a son, Walden. **FREDERICK ECKMANN** is a narrow-eyed, narrow-minded, treacherous provincial who lives in Bowling Green, Ohio—a verdant suburb of Thanatopsis. He doesn't write much, having had to teach courses like "American Literature from Plymouth Rock to Moby Dick" and having seen many of the atrocities wrought upon language by quondam heroes. If you feed him gin-and-tonic he domesticates easily and cuts out the snarls and the growls. He has a very nice wife, known, depending on mood, as either Miss Martha or Big Tex. I get a rumor that his useful survey of what has been happening in certain areas of our poetry since the Forties, *Cobras & Cockle-Shells,* is being reprinted by a university in Athens, Georgia. Lord God! **LARRY EIGNER** describes himself as a "non-disquisitious, non-Latinate, non-Classical (increasingly beat) non-reader—and I'd undoubtedly get lost in Dahlberg's neck of the woods if I ever made real time for the trip there." But the poem included in the *Festschrift* "kind of dropped on my head" while reading a review by Arno Karlen of *Reasons of the Heart.* Eigner lives in Swampscott, Massachusetts. His singular books of poems have been appearing since 1953—from Divers, Jargon, Coyote's Journal, Fulcrum, and Black Sparrow. **ARNOLD GASSAN** is a photographer, teaching rhetoric and dye-transfer these days at Ohio University in Athens and, in the summers, at the "Center for the Eye" in Aspen. He is known particularly for his photo-silk-screen experimentation. **BERNARD GOTFRYD** works for *Newsweek* magazine and has taken hundreds of photographs of Edward Dahlberg. The one I have selected for the frontispiece strikes me as the most revealing ever taken of E. D. **IHAB HASSAN** teaches at Wesleyan University in Middletown, Connecticut. His essay on De Sade appeared in *TriQuarterly* 15. **JOSE-PHINE HERBST** (1897–1969) was a forthright, intransigeant, very ignored writer of very much worth. Her proletarian novels of the Thirties are lost from sight now; in fact, perhaps her only work known currently is her book on John Bartram, *New Green World* (Hastings House). In the summer of 1967 she wrote: "I'm sorry to be so slow answering your request for current news of myself, but it bores me, all this kind of thing. In comparison to the jumping jacks omnipresent, I am a sluggard. I am still at work on my long book, a very complicated affair. . . . Otherwise it might be pertinent to mention my long essay about Dahlberg which ran in *Southern Review* and which I have been told is one of the best pieces of comprehensive criticism he has received." **ANSELM HOLLO** has been digging in the Buffalomoola and the Iowamoola mines of late and become distracted from his letter-writing—a pity since he is so expert at same. Two years ago his state was: "b. 1934 in Helsinki, Finland. Has lived in England since 1958, currently on the Isle of Wight (where a big white Persian cat is often seen sitting majestically on Swinburne's grave). Books (to mention a few I still like, myself): *Some Poems by Paul Klee*, & *It Is a Song, Faces and Forms, The Going-On Poem*. Forthcoming, poems and translations: *The Man in the Treetop Hat, Helsinki* (*Selected Poems of Pentti Saarikoski*), *Selected Poems of Paavo Haavikko* (Cape), and *Journey(s)*." **RONALD JOHNSON** is living in San Francisco. His most recent books of poems are these: *The Book of the Green Man* (Norton), *Valley of the Many-Colored Grasses* (Norton); *Balloons for Moonless Nights* and *Sports & Divertissements* (Finial Press); and *The Spirit Walks, The Rocks Will Talk* (Jargon Society). Mina Loy, paying him the greatest compliment possible to a Kansas poet, assured him his poems were "gracious to Buffalo." **SIMPSON KALISHER** works out of his New York studio on assignments all over the world. His best known book is *Railroad Men*, photographs and stories. When I was unable to reprint *Bottom Dogs*, I suggested it to Ferlinghetti, who brought out a City Lights paperback in 1961 with a portion of this same Kalisher photo used on the cover. **ARNO KARLEN**—what little I know about him comes in occasional bacchic revelations from poet Tim Reynolds, going back to the old days at Antioch College. When he wrote his contribution for the *Festschrift*, Mr. Karlen had just resigned from *Holiday* magazine. To my knowledge he now lives in New York City, free-lancing and working on a study of male sexuality, like they say. His contribution to the present opus seems very acute to me. **JAMES KEARNS,** the painter, lives in Dover, New Jersey. He made forty-two drawings for the New Directions edition of Dahlberg's *Can These Bones Live* (1960). Selden Rodman calls Kearns one of the "Insiders." I don't know what Colin Wilson and William F. Buckley call him. Times are hard enough. **ROBERT KELLY** is the Stately Pleasure Dome of American poetry, a veritable body of work, crammed with things like discrete information about Phineas Fletcher's *The Purple Island;* the rare knowledge that "art is perfected attention"; and such wise and unfashionable notions as that Delius' *A Mass of Life* is the greatest choral work of the century. ("One thinks of the popularity of Orff; I remember the story of Webern's being forced by the Gestapo to attend a performance of *Carmina Burana,* & to stand thru it.") Kelly teaches at Bard College, Annandale-on-Hudson. In discussing the *Festschrift* he wrote: "My only edge here wd be: in the scholarly hackademy, the Festschrift is certainly for Professor Horrendo Carramba, but it is not *abt* him; it is abt the things that interest him, or with wch he has dallied, Nerval's homard, Mallarmé's English grammar & so on. If the occasion ever arises, it might be instructive to try the same for a writer, & get his grateful or ingrate contemporaries & chillun to submit instances of their own work enlightened or shaped or copied from or influenced by, &c, the master to be honored. . . ." *The Common Shore* (Black Sparrow) is the latest of many books of poems. **HUGH KENNER** has one of those precision minds that make most cloudy poets plead for mercy and shelter. Yet this isn't arrogance— just the feeling that there is little in the language since Pound worth explicating and that you had better measure up. While he goes for the Literary Glaciers, he is kind enough to allow that I, for one, am an occasionally useful "Custodian of Snowflakes." Alors. His book on the sources of the *Cantos* promises to be as dazzling as Lord Peter Wimsey on the chase. Professor Kenner teaches at the University of California at Santa Barbara. **JACK KEROUAC** sent his spontaneous little offering to the *Festschrift* on a postal from Lowell, Mass., with a sort of john-wayne-type autograph under it in red ballpoint. **ANTHONY KERRIGAN** lives in Palma de Mallorca and in Dublin. I am familiar only with his translation of Garcia's *Chronicles of Florida.* He has been engaged for some time on the translation of *The Selected Works of*

Miguel de Unamuno. He writes: "Edward Dahlberg was the prime mover of the project to put Unamuno into English in nine volumes." **R. B. KITAJ,** originally of Chagrin Falls, Ohio (up the road from Crane's Canary Cottage, cor blimey), lives in London and in Oxford, and is represented by the Marlborough-Gerson Gallery in New York City. He is one of the most respected young painters in the world and has coined at least one already famous remark: "Books are my trees." Certainly few writers have read so much, or so seriously. A man of action. He rose from a plate of curry in a London restaurant one day and said we were flying immediately to Dublin. I said, why? He said, because Dahlberg was there and would know where the good books were in the shops. . . . His cover drawing was made expressly for the *Festschrift.* **JAMES LAUGHLIN** has been on the job at New Directions for an incredible 35 years, and has done more for more writers—difficult and otherwise—than anyone in the history of American letters. The world would long ago have been left to Rod McKuen, Anne Morrow Lindbergh, and poeticules who went to Yale or Harvard were it not for Laughlin. (Not to forget his mentor: Mr. Pound.) **DAVID LEVINE's** drawing is reprinted through the courtesy of the *New York Review of Books* and is copyright by them, 1968. **JAMES LOWELL,** of the Asphodel Book Shop, secured the photograph of the now-destroyed Jewish Orphan Asylum from the Cleveland Historical Society. My thanks to both parties. **WALTER LOWENFELS,** whose poetic achievement dates back to the 1920's, has passed his 70th birthday at full tilt and is living in Peekskill, New York. Jargon published Lowenfels' *Some Deaths (Selected Poems & Communications, 1925–1962)* in 1964. He is the editor of two recent anthologies: *Where Is Vietnam?* (Anchor) and *New Jazz Poets* (Folkways). The last I heard, Walter was working on the *Love Poems of Walt Whitman.* **FRANK MAC-SHANE** is on the staff of the Graduate Writing Program, School of the Arts, Columbia University. At one time he mentioned that he was commissioned to write a book about Dahlberg—what has happened to the plan I do not know. **JAMES MCGARRELL** teaches Graduate Painting at Indiana University, Bloomington. His drawing reproduced in the *Festschrift* was commissioned as a cover for Dahlberg's *Alms for Oblivion* when it seemed that Jargon would be its publisher instead of University of Minnesota Press. Allan Frumkin (Chicago and New York) is his principal dealer. A portfolio of McGarrell lithographs and my poems, *Sharp Tools for Catullan Gardens,* is still available from them.

188

THOMAS MCGRATH hides out with the crazy horses in places like Fargo, North Dakota, and Oneonta, New York, and because of it his poetry is much too little noticed. He has a number of books with Alan Swallow. He writes: "I remember reading *Bottom Dogs* somewhere in the farback and the sense of the book remained with me as one of the true witnesses of the times. Then, much later, I came upon a wholly new Dahlberg (or so it seemed to me) in a review of Aiken's *Ushant*. This is certainly one of the most remarkable reviews ever written—the load of classical reference and quotation hits like buckshot. This took me to some of the later work and to the poems, which seem to me very 'exotic,' certainly original and quite beautiful. I would like to know how Dahlberg manages this double mask or phoenix effect or whatever it is, because the problem (how to get beyond one's first matter and manner toward more mature work) is a prime one for American writers in particular." **RALPH EUGENE MEATYARD** is the dark visionary Gothic soul of Central Kentucky, hidden behind the front of kindly optician at "Eyeglasses of Kentucky" in a shopping center in Lexington. Gnomon Press is publishing a book on Meatyard this year. The *Festschrift* photograph was sent because "everyone always connects Dahlberg with barbershops from *Bottom Dogs* on." **THOMAS MERTON**'s death, by accident, in Bangkok in December 1968, terminated a unique career in American letters. It came during his only major trip away from the Abbey of Gethsemani in Trappist, Kentucky, in 25 years, and thus seems particularly ironic. And particularly sad. It seems appropriate to quote from his letters of 1967 regarding the *Festschrift:* "I am terribly sorry for the delay in writing. Doctors again, operation again, nonsense again, tests, inspections, inquisitions, visits of publishers, scrutinies of lawyers, quarrels of abbots, plagues of insects, bloody rain, dragons in the woods behind the shack, well diggers pounding the earth, varmints scampering, St. Elmo's fire in abundance, northern lights in the bedroom, incidence of leprosy in the mind—but *leprosy*. Poems of leprosy have followed the St. Elmo's fire and the unquietness of the age. . . . Now for Dahlberg! I haven't been anchoritic enough these last weeks, and it culminated in a big flap in Louisville when an old friend of mine was ordained priest at 60 in a sudden charismatic seizure of bishops. I went in and got stoned on champagne, which must have surprised the cult public. I am now hoping to get back into a little quiet, and meditation, and poetry. But meantime, I have been held up in writing the current curriculum. I am bad

189

at writing these things—'born on a chimney pot in Strasbourg in 1999, etc.' I hope you are having luck with the *Festschrift* contributions. I suppose it is understandable, though, that some people rebel at making statements that might sound like blurbs. There are too many statements about everything, and I am lucky to be out of the blizzard thereof, so can talk without embarrassment about liking, say, Dahlberg." . . . "Born 1915 in Southern France a few miles from Catalonia, so that I imagine myself by birth Catalan and am accepted as such in Barcelona where I have never been. Exiled, therefore, from Catalonia, I came to New York, then went to Bermuda, then back to France, then to school at Montauban, then to school at Oakham in England, to Clare College, Cambridge, where my scholarship was taken away after a year of riotous living, to Columbia University, New York, where I earned two degrees in Dullness and wrote a master's thesis on Blake. Taught English among Franciscan football players at St. Bonaventure University, and then became a Trappist monk at Gethsemani, Ky., in 1941. First published book of poems: 1944. Autobiography (1948) created a general hallucination followed by too many pious books. Back to poetry in the Fifties and Sixties. Gradual backing away from the monastic institution until I now live alone in the woods not claiming to be anything except, of course, a Catalan. But a Catalan in exile who would not return to Barcelona under any circumstances, never having been there. Have translated work of poets like Vallejo, Alberti, Hernandez, Nicanor Parra, etc. Proud of facial resemblance to Picasso and/or Jean Genet or alternately Henry Miller (though not so much Miller)." **PAUL METCALF,** whose great-grandfather wrote books with titles like *Moby-Dick* and *Billy Budd,* also lives in the Berkshires, on the eastern slope. Jargon has published two of his narratives, *Will West* (1956) and *Genoa: A Telling of Wonders* (1966). *Patagoni* comes next from his arcanum in the wild thyme. **THOMAS MEYER,** a recent graduate of Bard College, is amanuensis to the Jargon Society. He indicates: "This is a translation from 'Peri Didaxeon' ('Of the Schools of Medicine'), which appears in the third tome of *Leechdoms, Wortcunning & Starcraft of Early England,* edited by the Rev. Thomas Oswald Cockayne. This particular piece was translated into Old English about the 12th century and is a fine example of the language's degeneration." Mr. Meyer's first book of poems, *The Bang Book,* is being published this year by Jargon, illustrated by Peter Leventhal. **CHRIS-**

190

TOPHER MIDDLETON, discoverer of Pata-Xanadu, symbolist, most uninsular of recent British poets, was born in 1926 in Truro in Cornwall. Poems: *Torse 3* (1962), *Nonsequences* (1965). Translations: *Modern German Poetry* (1962), with Michael Hamburger; *German Writing Today* (Penguin, 1967); *The Walk and Other Stories,* by Robert Walser (1957). He has been living in the hills west of Austin, Texas, surrounded by armadillos and boat-tailed grackles, translating the letters of Nietzsche, plus Walser's third novel, *Jakob von Gunten.* **HERBERT MILLER** is a professor in one of the New York City colleges, and was a student of Edward Dahlberg's in 1947 at Boston University. **FRED MORAMARCO** has written a book on Edward Dahlberg for Twayne's United States Authors Series. He is now teaching at San Diego State College; and continues as an editor of the *Western Humanities Review,* based at the University of Utah. **ERIC MOTTRAM** lectures at the University of London on American literature and includes Dahlberg in a course, "Self and Community in America," along with Paul Goodman, Henry Miller, Burroughs, Thoreau, and others. Mr. Mottram comes from the Isle of Wight and lives in Kensington, London, where his Berlioz, Messiaen, Ives, and Berio records are played with un-English fervor. **GILBERT NEIMAN** has settled down in the woods near Clarion, Pennsylvania, and tries, like the rest of us, not to get shot. "I'm a poet and novelist; the Ph.D.'s a screen. Or a scream." He is best known for his novel, *There's a Tyrant in Every Country,* much praised by Henry Miller and Anais Nin. **PHILIP O'CONNOR,** a regular at The George, near the BBC in London, writes poems, autobiography (*Memoirs of a Public Baby, Living in Croesor*), on vagrancy in England (Penguins), etc., etc. When he last wrote he was living near Newmarket in Suffolk, suffering the English literary life rather gloomily. **WILLIAM O'ROURKE** is presently attending the Columbia Writers' School and finishing a novel. **JOEL OPPENHEIMER** (certainly the worst softball pitcher in the history of Black Mountain College—but also certainly the funniest) operates under a tacky fur hat in some bar on the west side of the Village. Few people have ever been there except New Yorkers who have never been to the United States. He has lived as a printer and typographer and ran projects for a time at St. Mark's Church-in-the-Bowery. In 1970 he is publishing two books of poems, with Bobbs-Merrill and with the Jargon Society. He has two earlier books and a play, *The Great American Desert* (Grove). One of Yahweh's last real Yankee folks. **DONALD J. PAQUETTE** sends this rueful account of life: "A forlorn and fatherless waif who once helped make democracy safe for the world and was thrown for a bloody loss. A true lover of Keats, Ecclesiastes, the Rimbaud of Cwmdonkin Drive, Simplicity, and the Ambidextrous Adjective. A prairie wordsmith, lost in the Black Forest of Obscurity and Abstraction, who has been trying for 40 years to make a good poem and—almost succeeded." **NORMAN HOLMES PEARSON** suggests: "Why not simply say that I am, or have been (has-been?), 'an anthologist, reviewer, and teacher.' If you like your contributors in Sunday-go-to-Meeting clothes, however, I guess everything revelant is in *Who's Who in America,* which, like the obituary page of the *New York Times,* is careful to include respectable academics." *The Oxford Book of American Literature,* which Mr. Pearson edited with William Rose Benét back in the Thirties, has always struck me as a model of its kind. **HAROLD ROSENBERG** I've always thought of as the "Apollinaire of New York"—something about his head and his carriage, something about his preeminence, lonely and enduring, over an island of aesthetes, many of whom should have been rug merchants. He is now art critic of *The New Yorker;* professor of the Committee on Social Thought at the University of Chicago; and program consultant of the Advertising Council. Two of his best known books are *The Anxious Object* and *The Tradition of the New.* A book of poems, *Trance Above the Streets,* was published in 1942. **IRVING ROSENTHAL** used to edit *Big Table* in Chicago, which used to print Dahlberg in some pretty strange company (Mr. Burroughs, for one) and stirred up an unexpected audience for him in a number of Beat writers and readers. It was not long afterward that *Esquire* published one of its charts showing where it was at amongst writer-fellers. Dahlberg was in the top three in the Jolly Gray Guru Division. . . . I remember meeting Rosenthal for the first time with Allen Ginsberg one day in the Village (1958). We went to see Dahlberg in his tiny room in the famous, seedy Marlton Hotel; then repaired to some apartment owned by ladies of the First Zen Institute to eat delicatessen and drink beer. The ladies were wearing bone jewelry and squatting on air mattresses. It was a comical scene—Dahlberg trading insults with the neophytes formerly with Mary Baker Eddy and Gurdjieff in Montclair, New Jersey. . . . Rosenthal has since published a novel, *Sheeper* (Grove), and lives in San Francisco. **RAYMOND ROSENTHAL's**

192

contribution first appeared as a review in *The Nation*. All I know about the gentleman is that he was the editor of an anthology, *McLuhan: Pro & Con* (Funk & Wagnalls). **MURIEL RUKEYSER's** distinguished career includes such books of poems as *Waterlily Fire, Body of Waking, The Green Wave, If Turning Wind,* back to *Theory of Flight* in the Thirties. The present poem appeared in *The Speed of Darkness* (Random House, 1968). Miss Rukeyser has written prose books on Willard Gibbs and Thomas Hariot. **WILLIAM RYAN** is in the Department of English at the University of Missouri at Kansas City. I know little about him otherwise, except his passion for William Langland's work, and the following: "I was a Mississippi River Rat (forgive the expression, o friend of E. D.) for 25 years, in northern Iowa, and even now I spend one third of my time in the country, usually 3–5 days at a stretch on a boat on the Lake of the Ozarks. December to April I don't leave the slip but the scenery is good even so." **AUBREY SCHWARTZ** lives in Sag Harbor, New York. He is known primarily for his etchings, lithographs, and drawings. His bronze portrait-bust of Edward Dahlberg represents a lesser known facet of his work. **EDWIN SEAVER,** editor-in-chief of George Braziller, Inc., is the editor of *Epitaphs of Our Times: The Letters of Edward Dahlberg.* In the 1940's Mr. Seaver initiated and edited the four volumes of *Cross Section,* an annual of new writing, in which he published the first works of a number of American writers who have since become well known, among others Arthur Miller's play, *The Man Who Had All the Luck,* and Norman Mailer's "work in progress," *The Naked and the Dead.* He is also the author of two novels published in the Thirties, *The Company* and *Between the Hammer and the Anvil,* concerning which he writes us: "If any of our readers has one or both of these books and can bear parting with them (which should entail no great sacrifice), I would like to buy them as I do not have a copy of either book myself." **KARL SHAPIRO's** words are from his review of *Epitaphs of Our Times,* published in the "Book Week" section of the *New York World Journal Tribune* on February 5, 1967. When last in touch, Shapiro was teaching at the University of Illinois at Chicago Circle. **ADELE Z. SILVER** writes a genial letter, but I know nothing about the lady except that she wrote a piece in the *Cleveland Plain Dealer* (April 23, 1967), "Father of Beatnik Novel 'Discovered'," from which I have taken excerpts for the *Festschrift.* The class picture of Dahlberg in 1917 at the Jewish Orphan Asylum came from Mrs. Silver's story, and we thank her also for that discovery. **ART SINSABAUGH,** occasionally accused of being a blind Venetian photographer, sent his print with a small note: "May Mr. Dahlberg learn to understand photographs!" Sinsabaugh provided the superb Midwestern landscapes for Jargon's edition of Sherwood Anderson's *Six Mid-American Chants,* for which Dahlberg provided a note. He teaches at the University of Illinois, Urbana. **AARON SISKIND** taught English in New York high schools before becoming one of our most conspicuous photographers in the Thirties and later instructing so ably at Black Mountain, the Institute of Design (Chicago), and elsewhere. He writes: "I met Dahlberg years ago at George Cavallon's, & he was arguing with John Cage. I can think of no living literary person we have *needed* more." Siskind's photograph "Rome Hieroglyph: Homage to Edward Dahlberg" is dated 1963. He lives in Chicago. **GILBERT SORRENTINO** was born in Brooklyn in 1929. Contrary to popular opinion, Brooklyn is not a funny place. He survived his childhood, and at about the age of 17 began writing poems in what he thought was a Poundian manner. Heeding the call of Duty, he was drafted into the Army, where he served an undistinguished two years as a medic, winning neither medals nor praise. He is the author of three books of poems: *The Darkness Surrounds Us* (Jargon), *Black and White* (Totem/Corinth), and *The Perfect Fiction* (Norton); and one novel, *The Sky Changes* (Hill & Wang). He presently lives and works in New York City, where he spends most of his time refuting the bourgeois canard that steady employment is good for the artist. His feeling for Dahlberg is clear and direct: "There are not many men around who persist like that in the head." **ALLEN TATE**'s eminence as a critic and poet requires no encapsulating. Mr. Tate is living again at Sewanee, Tennessee, in residence at the University of the South. **KIM TAYLOR** is English, born in India. He has wandered widely and done many things, including a stint at the University of Texas in Austin teaching book design and Oriental art and ideas. He has edited and designed magazines and the books of the Art Press (Marazion, Cornwall). Under the pseudonym Michael Adam, he has written *The Labour of Love* and *A Matter of Death & Life.* He now lives in Somerset, near Dulverton. **JOHN WAIN,** who is more ebullient and garrulous than any ten well-sloshed supporters of the Manchester United football team, is likewise enmeshed in a dozen literary things at once, all with tight deadlines. He has been producing well over one book a year for the past 15 years—fiction, autobiography, criticism, essays, poetry. More important, he gets better all the time and needs to live until 80 to get it all done. **VICTOR WEYBRIGHT** will publish an edition of "literary portraits" by Dahlberg sometime in the next few years. **PHILIP WHALEN** is one of the few poets of my generation, as Rexroth might say, I'd care to sit next to on a bus, or take a walk with, like Basho. I don't often get the chance since he stays mostly in Kyoto, San Francisco, and the Pacific ranges, and I have given up on most places west, or east, of the Appalachians. His big book of poems, *At Bear's Head* (Harcourt), belongs in any literate hiking pack, along with Gilbert White or Marston Bates or the *Loon Trilogy*. **EDWARD KEITH WHITTAKER** is presently unemployed and any job offers may be forwarded through this office. His interest in Dahlberg has led him into a further study of the life-styles and myths of North American Indians. He lives in Timmins, Ontario. **THEODORE WILENTZ** was for many years co-owner of the Eighth Street Bookshop in Greenwich Village, the only shop in the country where most of the clerks had doctorates and Guggenheims and wrote in *The Nation* on Nabokov and Mina Loy. He is now director of publications for the Sierra Club and the publisher of Corinth Books. Ted says, "You may characterize me as you wish"—which gives me the welcome opportunity of stating publicly that there are few men more conspicuous for their love of writing and for their support over the years of writers and poets in need of friendship. **KEITH WILSON** is a dug-in member of the arcane "Rio Grande Renaissance" and lives in a small Spanish-American village near Las Cruces, where he teaches at New Mexico State University. I keep waiting to see that book of his from Grove Press. **DOUGLAS WOOLF** continues his wanderings in remote towns of the West (Langley, Washington, is the latest) and continues to write his outrageously ignored fiction. Jargon Society is publishing a book of his this year; so is Harper's. I remember him vividly, selling Good Humors in Pueblo, Colorado, and living in a shack next to the American Oyster Factory near Tacoma. It takes a lot to write books as good as *Fade Out* and *Wall to Wall*. **JONATHAN WILLIAMS,** to end with myself, is living in Upper Wharfedale in the West Riding of Yorkshire, having forsaken Strom Thurmond, Jerry

Rubin, and Marshall McLuhan for a diet of rusticated mildew and William Morris. My last position was as poet-in-residence at the Maryland Institute of Art in Baltimore. I am finishing a book on hiking in Great Britain, and have published several recent books of poems: *Strung Out with Elgar on a Hill* (Finial Press), *Mahler* (Cape Goliard/ Grossman), *Slowowls* (Cape Goliard/Grossman), with Ronald Johnson, and *An Ear in Bartram's Tree* (University of North Carolina Press), which would probably sell better as *A Queer on Batman's Knee,* the times being what they are. . . . I am director of the Jargon Society, based at Penland School in the North Carolina mountains. To quote Dahlberg: "I don't know what I'm doing, but continue to do it." I must have made many errors in compiling this list of contributors, but indulgence is again asked, because (1) the seas are running very high, (2) there is not even a paperback dictionary on the ship, (3) the Bols gin is marvelously cheap, and (4) I am surrounded by Midianites, Laodiceans, cordial Dutchmen, Plastic Hydrangea People, and jabbering admirals' wives from Jacksonville, who make the editing of a *Festschrift* seem an odd business indeed.